School of Errors

School of Errors

Rethinking School Safety in America

David P. Perrodin
Foreword by Danny Woodburn

ROWMAN & LITTLEFIELD
Lanham • Boulder • New York • London

Published by Rowman & Littlefield
An imprint of The Rowman & Littlefield Publishing Group, Inc.
4501 Forbes Boulevard, Suite 200, Lanham, Maryland 20706
www.rowman.com

6 Tinworth Street, London SE11 5AL

British Library Cataloguing in Publication Information Available

Library of Congress Cataloging-in-Publication Data

Names: Perrodin, David P., author.
Title: School of errors : rethinking school safety in America / David P. Perrodin.
Description: Lanham : Rowman & Littlefield, [2019] | Includes bibliographical references and index.
Identifiers: LCCN 2019014668 (print) | LCCN 2019022203 (ebook) | ISBN 9781475837445 (cloth : alk. paper) | ISBN 9781475837469 (electronic)
Subjects: LCSH: Schools--United States--Safety measures. | Emergency management--United States. | School crisis management--United States.
Classification: LCC LB2864.5 .P47 2019 (print) | LCC LB2864.5 (ebook) | DDC 371.7/820973--dc23
LC record available at https://lccn.loc.gov/2019014668
LC ebook record available at https://lccn.loc.gov/2019022203

Contents

Praise for *School of Errors*   ix

Foreword   xiii
   Danny Woodburn

Preface: Shooting Rubber Bullets   xvii

Acknowledgments: Member Checks   xxv

Introduction: School Safety in America   1

Part I: The Torus   **15**

  1 How Thinking about a Bagel Can Get You through the Worst Day
     of Your Life   17

  2 Exploration Is a Kind of Safety Drill   25

  3 Situational Awareness via Sensemaking, Your Sword and Shield   29

  4 Legacy Knowledge   33

Part II: The Foolishness of Benchmarking   **37**

  5 Disasters Are the Real Snowflakes   39

  6 Another New Latin Word: Psychological Transference   43

  7 So What's Wrong with Benchmarking?: Critical Decision-
     Making in a Nonlinear World   49

  8 Why Comparing Disasters Feels Too Good to Be True   53

  9 One Variable, One Very Big Difference: The Internet   55

10 A Final Word on Schools and Benchmarking   57

Part III: Drill Fidelity   **59**

11 Fancy Drills Are Worse than Useless   63

12 The Right Way to Conduct a Drill: Critical Decision-Making in a Nonlinear World   69

13 Other Options: Tabletop Exercises and Focus Groups   73

14 What Is a Tabletop Exercise?   77

15 Video Boondoggle   81

16 One More Don't: Professional Standards for Educational Leaders   85

Part IV: Systems Will Develop, So Let Them   **89**

17 The Zen of Safety   91

18 Incident Command Structure   93

19 Tornadoes, Hurricanes, and the Fabulous Cajun Navy Relief   99

20 Seeing Faces on the Moon: How Pareidolia Helped the Rescue System on 9/11 Develop   103

21 Transitioning into Chaos: How Increasing the "Noise" Increases Options . . . Up to a Point   105

22 Hobbes's Leviathan Meets the Twin Towers   109

Part V: How We Know What We Know   **117**

23 Simulated Annealing: How the Human Brain Is Specialized for Improvisation   119

24 Leadership Theories After Hobbes   125

25 Legacy Knowledge, Distributed Leadership, and Rookie Teachers vs. Admiral Loy   129

26 Summary of What We Know   137

27 How Will Decisions Made in the Moment Be Studied? And How Will Future Decisions Be Directed?   139

28 Bollards and Planters: The Terrible Ideas That Are Coming to a School Near You   145

29 A Mile Wide and an Inch Deep   153

30 Final Implications for School Leaders   157

Epilogue: Nothing Means Anything to Anyone Until It Means Everything to You   161

References   165

Index   169

About the Author 177

Praise for *School of Errors*

THE MOST *HONEST* BOOK *EVER* WRITTEN ABOUT THE
$3 BILLION #SCHOOLSAFETY INDUSTRIAL COMPLEX!

"Over the last 20 years, in the wake of unthinkable school shootings, school safety has propelled itself to priority number one for school leaders. A priority that has not had the thoughtful support of understanding what we need to do to address the simple question, 'What if?' A question with an endless number of scenarios which we honestly struggle to reasonably counter. We spend countless amounts of resources of time and money to fortify our schools and train our staff. Yet intuitively we sense we are somehow possibly missing the boat. David allows us a moment to step back and thoughtfully reconsider the landscape before us."

   —**Mati Palm-Leis**, superintendent, School District of Mellen Wisconsin

"Dr. David Perrodin gives the reader a contrarian view on the current school security establishment. The emphasis is placed more on the individual for timely action than it does bollard fencing. Perrodin's *School of Errors* puts you in the front row of active shooter crime scenes. What is needed and how to survive them."

   —**Thomas Marchetti**, retired Los Angeles Police Detective

"If you have any interest in saving kids' lives, you need this book. It's not a regurgitation of the 'hide-run-fight' mantra, but a deeper study of what humans do in chaotic, unpredictable emergencies and how to apply those lessons. We say that, 'An ounce of prevention is worth a pound of cure.' In real life that means it is cheaper, easier, and more effective to spot troubled students than to spend millions on 'security bling' that we already know doesn't work. Better to cultivate a principles-based flexible attitude than memorize a dozen rigid, impossibly specific responses that only work in the unlikely event that your chaos matches a previous chaos. David Perrodin gives you a way to think about the problem and an insight into how the humans you deal with are probably going to handle it anyway, so you can work with nature instead of trying to script the unpredictable."

—**Rory Miller**, author, *Meditations on Violence*

"Dr. Perrodin boldly reveals the internal mechanisms of the billion dollar school safety industry in his must-read book *School of Errors*. As a school district administrator in elementary education, the safety of my students and staff is a matter of the utmost importance. David untangles the issues all school leaders face from years of vague policy guidance, unchecked fortification, and a complete absence of accessible design for safety instruction and threat reporting systems. Students have been pushed to the sidelines of safety. *School of Errors* is the overdue invitation to America's youth that they are crucially needed to inform the practices and systems that promote the safety of *their* school environment. This book will immediately change how you think about school safety!"

—**Missy Herek**, elementary principal, Hillsboro School District, Hillsboro, Wisconsin

"David Perrodin adeptly tackles and untangles a topic that is on everyone's minds these days—keeping schools safe—with blunt honesty and keen insight drawn from years of experience. The book debunks the many 'quick fix' solutions that do nothing but drain taxpayer dollars in exchange for a facile illusion of safety. Dr. Perrodin's goal is to instead urge all involved to look at the problem from a sober, realistic viewpoint and pursue safety strategies that emphasize flexibility, common sense, and the ability to assess how things actually work in the real world. There is no other book like it available today, making it a must-read for both parents and experts alike."

—**Mike Valentino**, editor, *Jersey Joe Walcott: A Boxing Biography*

"Dr. Perrodin's book guides us back to true prevention. Millions of dollars are being spent on fortifying our schools, when possibly the assailant might already be behind the walls. School safety should be focused on mental health services, reporting tools, improving school climate, and threat assessment training."

—**Salvador Arias**, safe schools coordinator, Kern County, California

"School safety has been an enigma to school officials and parents alike. Misguided solutions presented by the mainstream media have provoked us into implementing knee-jerk practices in response to school tragedies. Dr. David Perrodin's book provides a steadfast approach, removing the rhetoric while providing clear focused guidance on understanding school safety and the tools needed to implement guided adaptive critical thinking during chaotic emergency situations. School officials, as well as parents, would benefit greatly from reading this book."

—**Hector Solis**, creator and host, *Awareness Podcast*

"In *School of Errors*, David Perrodin offers comprehensive, practical expertise around school safety. Following some bullying complaints and behavior incidents a few years ago, we hired David as a consultant during a review of district safety operational systems. Under his advisement, and vetted through research and his own field experiences, our district revamped its procedures. Based on student-centered needs, the evidence-based practices (emphasizing prevention, restoration, and accountability) were so relevant that our district continues to use them today. With adverse social and mental health issues on the rise in our country, school personnel will find David's message to be just the right antidote. Read his book and start the work! Time is critical and our children deserve nothing less."

—**Cynthia Russell Smith**, director, Student Services, Marinette School
District, Marinette, Wisconsin

"School district administrators face an uphill battle when it comes to ensuring safe schools for their students, staff, and families. *School of Errors* gives schools a road map for navigating the gauntlet of challenges around school safety. Dr. David Perrodin delivers research-tested, relevant strategies for creating and sustaining safe schools."

—**Joe Bruzzese**, CEO, Sprigeo

"At a time when public awareness of school safety is at an all-time high, Dr. David Perrodin's *School of Errors* provides practical, evidence-based wisdom. School administrators will be well-served to peruse these pages before giving into pressure to purchasing costly safety equipment or developing complex safety procedures."

—**Michele Butler**, principal, Arcadia Middle School, Arcadia, Wisconsin

"As a parent of two children with special needs, I often have specific questions about school safety. What are my children being taught about safety? What do they *actually* understand about safety and reporting threats? How does the safety plan work when somebody is absent? Administrators assure parents that schools are safe. Yet we know from our own experiences that during a crisis, something will happen and scripted plans will be hurled out the window. Then what? Dr. Perrodin gives us the expert insight of someone who can answer that question. I highly recommend you read *School of Errors* and *really* let it all sink in."

—**Tabatha Malliard**, parent of two children with special needs,
Pennsylvania

Foreword

Danny Woodburn

Dr. David Perrodin's book has a universal importance that extends beyond one institution, beyond one focus. There is an overreaching social significance that not only can every parent grab ahold of but also every person who has an interest in any child's future. It's not about special needs for a select few but special needs for the community as a whole.

In the 1960s and 1970s my mother met every kind of ignorance imaginable, having one son with dwarfism (Spondyloepiphyseal Dysplasia Congenita, SED) and another son, my brother Steven, with Down syndrome. Having a single mom who dealt daily with stares, snickers, slurs, institutional obstacles, and much worse showed me what it meant to have an advocate. Back in 2010, I gave a keynote for RespectABILITY Coalition of California. At that time, I had been active in the disability community as a proponent of inclusion and employment of persons with disabilities in film and television and the need for social change for many years. In that speech, I spoke for the first time of how I learned such advocacy from my mother. I learned first to advocate for myself but also saw what it meant for my brother to have an advocate.

As my career in show business grew, I saw the kinds of obstacles I was up against in terms of the types of roles I was offered. I'm not speaking about the fantastical elves, gnomes, aliens, etc. but more the offensive tropes about Little People that writers found amusing: the self-hatred, the pathetic nature of our existence, the dwarf as object, the overexaggerated dwarf libido that even had one character in a children's sit-com making sexual overtures to a fourteen-year-old—pedophilia as a source for comic gold (a role I promptly turned down, with objection). I saw how my own advocacy could extend the life and quality of my career with the kinds of choices and objections I made, especially after I gained some notoriety and recognizability.

I joined the SAG-AFTRA Performers With Disability Committee (PWD) and discovered the kinds of obstacles I faced were nothing compared to the prejudices, ignorance, and literal physical barriers that kept my colleagues from opportunity, employment, and the inclusive arena my industry raves about. I realized that these kinds of barriers in my industry extend to every industry, every institution, every possible social setting.

My deeper interaction with the disabled community, my community, has been enlightening. It has given me perspectives I did not have before. Going to an audition for a character in a wheelchair in which the casting office was on the second floor with no elevator access showed me the closed door to our community. It was engagement with that community that was the catalyst for my changed perspective.

Power players in the world of film and television inclusion have told me that the goal, for now, is acknowledging the need for cultural or gender diversity. Even with numbers showing the disparity for PWDs, the rhetoric is still exclusive. As we are sidelined in this discussion, I understand that rhetoric leads to policy being formed, which in turn leads to laws getting passed. This shows a lack of understanding of the fact that disability is inherently a culture as well. My interactions with other people with disability show me that we share a common thread in our experiences just like any culture.

I met David at one of the largest engagements of the disabled community, the 2017 International Inclusion Summit hosted by the Ruderman Family Foundation. David and I have continued discussions and perspectives of our various fields and have educated one another on subjects we previously knew very little about. But just as in my field, the objections to his perspective are also built on populist ideas, financial objectives, and ignorance. For David to tackle institutional practices that are inherently exclusive beyond the Americans with Disabilities Act (ADA) and the Individuals with Disabilities Education Act (IDEA) laws is seemingly insurmountable. This book pushes bigger ideas of inclusivity that can literally save lives.

It brings to mind the thought of what is legal versus what is equal. In my employment-seeking environment it is legal to hold auditions in a building that is pre-ADA compliance laws. It is legal to have programs that benefit people of color (PoC), women, and the LGBTQ community and call them inclusive and diverse yet still remain exclusive. It is legal to create laws that incentivize productions to hire PoC, women, and LGBTQ but not PWD.

This happens across many industries. In New York City, there is a contractors benefits program designed to help PoC and women but not disabled vets who may have been contractors prior to active duty and find it difficult to find work in their field. Although this rings of inequality and even blatant prejudice, it is perfectly legal. In fact there are even times when ADA laws are used for exclusion by preventing the industry from including the disabled workforce numbers in studies for fear of litigation—a completely unfounded fear but still rife with legal loopholes.

As David explains it, in his world there are programs set up to help children, students with disability, get an education per the laws in place (ADA, IDEA) that help with child education. Oftentimes these laws are the extent of the approach taken. As a result, the trap of what is legal versus what is equal returns to do damage to the potential future of these children. School boards may cite a fear of litigation by parents of children with disabilities who are included in school events and activities because of their own lack of understanding of the needs of that particular child.

Any advocate for any cause can attest that engagement is the key to change. As I have mentioned, my own engagement was the catalyst for my own changed perspectives beyond the self-interests of my career. Even though the industry has largely exempted itself from that engagement and thus legally limited PWDs' right to equal access to education, opportunity, and employment, I pursue the engagement, at risk to my own future, the need for change.

David's advocacy, not without risk, reinforces the idea that such engagement means understanding, looking at new ways to approach the subject of protecting our children. Engagement with inclusion yields a better result in protecting the lives of children across the board, not just those with special needs. The concept of successes built on engaging with a community is not new, but within the context of disability they are often overlooked out of ignorance, fear, and financial pursuits of those outside the institutions in need of engagement.

Dr. David Perrodin's book is a tremendous resource and guide on the issues of understanding safety as a whole and the safety of our children in institutions of learning. It is also a template for community engagement to create a more inclusive society within the very fabric of those that will make up that future society.

—Danny Woodburn

Credit: Bradford Rogne.

Danny Woodburn is a veteran actor who has worked on more than thirty films (*Mirror Mirror*, *Watchmen*, *Death to Smoochy*) and made more than 150 television appearances (*Seinfeld*, *Bones*, *Bold and the Beautiful*). He is a public speaker and activist on the subject of disability employment and inclusion, appearing on CNN, MSNBC, *CBS Sunday Morning*, and National Public Radio.

Preface

Shooting Rubber Bullets

As vitally important as school safety is, most of the professionals' recommendations on the subject of getting kids out of danger when a disaster occurs are dangerously wrong. This is a book about school safety and disaster readiness, but it's also a dangerous book to write . . . or at least it would be for me as an author and safety professional were I not currently sitting in a very good position for telling the truth.

I have spent a long time working and studying in both large and small schools in Wisconsin, as well as at the university level. My home state is a rural one. You wouldn't think of our schools as particularly dangerous—but we *do* have a long history of producing serial killers, forest fires, and polar bear plunge enthusiasts.

I got into this work by enjoying the boring stuff. I like the boxes of data, finding patterns, spotting details, and contributing to smarter systems. I have been the director of student services for small and large school districts in Wisconsin; I have worked with tiny facilities and with entire states. I've worked with safety companies to help distill data and develop efficient user-interface systems—or how students, parents, and staff report threats.

I did my Doctorate of Philosophy in educational leadership and policy analysis at Madison, the flagship school of the University of Wisconsin system. Awarded back-to-back research fellowships, I devoted two years, full time, to researching high-stakes safety decisions in education, health care, and the military. I've instructed university courses in school safety; I created, wrote, and starred in a PBS special on school safety; I run a podcast dedicated to school safety; and I've even written a film about school safety with Pulitzer Prize–winner David Obst.

Now I am ready to retire. I'm going to point out the problems that are easy to ignore, and I will be brutally honest with you about how we can fix them. I'm going to tell it like it is. *The empirical research does not support what most school safety experts are doing.* You want to know why these drills in which they fire soft pellets are ludicrous? I'm your guy. If you want to know why, if the weather had been worse on 9/11, the entire harbor rescue would have gone to the dogs, keep reading. If you are simply interested in the world of safety training and design, this may be your jam for a few hours.

Many of my colleagues pay no heed to studies, facts, and the lessons of historical disaster rescues such as 9/11, as well as the characteristics of modern students. Instead, they follow trends supported by zero evidence. Yet they are approved by the rest of the industry. Why? Office politics, political ideology, cash cows—and the inertia that occurs when people in an area of study are afraid to rock the boat. They've all become experts in trusting the experts that aren't necessarily experts.

This is understandable. Many went into the game presumably because they had an interest in helping people. But because of the same human interpersonal dynamics that make disaster studies complex and counterintuitive, they found that their living, their money—the clothes on their back, the food they put in their own kids' mouths—all depends on not being the person who swims against the tide.

Such a mentality is harmful. They are advocating spending vast amounts of public and donation money on programs that are supported by no reliable data, merely popular ideas. It's not just about the money, however; the time spent on this training is time not spent on better teaching and learning, better content knowledge, better systems design, and better wellness development. They ignore ideas that more powerfully describe reality and our best possibilities for protecting children and preparing them to survive the unthinkable.

I've seen former truth seekers in the field drop off one by one; people who used to stick to evidence-based ideas and established literature are suddenly saying, "Sure, run drills where you shoot rubber bullets at the students, that sounds like a good article for the local paper." These propped up strategies are worse than ineffective; they prepare us for failure in the terrible situations that we are trying to avoid. They are rubber ideas that may still have impact but will never have the impact of positive, preventative, effective safety training and preparation.

FIREFIGHTING IN DRESS SHOES AND $100,000 CAMERAS

Let me be clear. There's *no* evidence supporting the efficacy of hyper-realistic drills, someone just thought that sounded good. A takeaway from this book, by the way, will be that overly specific training doesn't help. And if I may use my own instincts for a moment, I think these approaches are just going to freak them out—or worse, *train them* for events where they can take a turn to shoot.

Safety professionals don't want to rock the boat because they make their living rowing it in the wrong direction. Their view is warped by pressure—many of them want to be good people, but they have to support their living via the industry. So they either have to remain silent or say they agree with solutions that are not evidence based. They are not ready to retire.

The safety ideas that work are usually the cheapest—the big price tags are statistically useless or worse. Instead of blowing the budget on metal detectors, train your staff on systems and awareness.

That's my specialty. I'm not going to sell you on expensive cameras, and I am not an expert on magic solutions; my field of study in recent years has been hive minds and the levers that can move them. I'm the guy who will tell you the often ugly facts about the way people work and specific reasons systems do things wrong.

I am also the guy whose advice about safety comes from a combination of both study and real-life experience in the field. You'll excuse me while I pause to brush my knuckles on my shirt with false modesty, but for a PhD, I've gotten pretty down and dirty. Let me tell you a story.

My favorite part of my career is teaching and interacting with students, but I also do a lot of grinding through reports, particularly when it comes to gigs in which I have to help lawyers bring the hammer down on a facility that is neglecting student safety. There will be weeks of fine-tooth combing for data screw-ups and thousands of hours spent with my nose in a file—but one must still be ready for anything. (This is true not just of my job, but of life. More on this later. *Much* more.)

One of my jobs that was highest on the desk jockey scale was at a medical facility. One day there, I was minding my own business—as we usually are when our reality explodes—doing some boring paperwork. I was fatigued and beginning to droop when I glanced up at the window and was suddenly very wide awake: rapidly approaching the facility through the brush was a massive prairie fire, binge eating its way through the adjacent field and belching smoke and flame. *Oh, nuts*, I thought. *Didn't see that one coming.*

I had almost zero time to make a decision. Large flames were hardly an unfamiliar problem to me though. I told you I've been around: I was a firefighter during the 1990s; I know fires, and I've had hundreds of hours of training and experience. I knew the local fire department was volunteer and chances were they would need help—both numbers-wise and from someone with a bit more experience than the average small town volunteer.

So without a second's thought—dressed in full business attire, including suit, dress shoes, button-up shirt, the whole works—I started sprinting out of the building to meet the fire department.

Sure enough, the only vehicle that appeared at first was a brush truck manned by a single eighteen-year-old volunteer firefighter. One guy! A kid! Ouch. Well, I made it two. I jumped on the back of the truck and was bounced across the deep ruts of a plowed field as my new right-hand man sped us toward the fire, my coattails flapping behind me. It must have made quite a sight.

The driver was young with limited experience, but he was trained and smart. He knew enough to start laying down a wet line with the hose, and I pulled up a special tarp that's used to drag along the edge of the burning area and smother the flames. In short, we did what people do in an emergency: we created a temporary system together that worked.

A lot of safety officials these days are obsessed with having systems in place, with binders full of flowcharts for every possible situation to make sure no one ever has to use their discretion.

Well, you know what that poet said about the best laid plans of mice and men. We all know deep down that they're going to go haywire the minute they smash up against reality. But it makes people feel better to have them, "just in case."

In that instance, there was no system in place—just a truck and two guys who had never met. And it came out textbook perfect. I hate to say it was magic, but it was an incredible experience. The answers effortlessly came to us. We communicated via hand signals and nods of the head as though we had a Vulcan mind meld.

When I got back to the facility, I found the soles of my dress shoes had melted off completely without my noticing it. I laughed; I must have been in what popular psychiatry calls a "flow state," in which my entire world was reduced to the task at hand. But that flow state included my spontaneous connection with my young comrade.

As I will discuss later, as amazing as it felt, this experience was not unique. Successful responses are always built around teams of people that are aware and ready to act. The episode illustrates one of the basic truths I want to drive home with this book. People with some knowledge and the desire to cooperate will create a system. Programs and policies rarely have the effect we think they will in the moment. We are rarely wearing the "right shoes for the job." Throughout the book, I'll bring stories that consistently show competent, rational, clear-thinking decision-making is our best safety resource.

Here's another example. I was at my desk around 5:00 p.m. winnowing papers and emails when a call came in from a colleague on the other side of the state. For me, he has always been what is called a "member check"—one of a handful of people I would run things past for an honest opinion. "David, we've got a school board meeting tonight," he told me, "and they're voting on a proposal to purchase a hundred thousand dollars' worth of surveillance cameras for the school. This isn't sitting well with me."

My colleague is sharp, and his uneasy feeling was rational. Surveillance cameras in schools are merely forensic tools—they're for after the smoke has cleared. They can tell you which kids were in that fight or who broke into Jimmy's locker. They are not, however, tools that will prevent or deescalate a school shooting.

He admitted: "The cameras are incredible. The vendor performed demos and you can put a camera in the gymnasium rafters and zoom in and read a newspaper held by someone on the floor."

I cut in. "That sounds impressive, but do you need this stuff? How's your two-way digital radio communications? That's where I would spend the money."

He paused. "There wasn't a study, David. I don't know the status of our radios. I know we don't have enough of them, and the principals complain that there are dead spots in the buildings, but I don't know all the details." He continued, saying, "The vendor claims that the new surveillance system could be accessed by police in their cars as they are speeding to a school to confront a shooter. Is that possible?"

It only took me a second to answer that. I have drilled with entry teams in full gear and arrived in a speeding squad car that jumped a curb and bounced to a stop. "No way in hell that will ever happen," I said. "First, the typical school shooting is completed in eight minutes. So to think that the cameras will track the shooter throughout the building—nope, it doesn't work that way. Yeah, Columbine was an exception—Denver SWAT didn't enter the building for hours—but my guess is that this will never be used by police responding to an active shooter call."

My colleague took my advice and stood his ground. He had the professional rapport to get the superintendent to side with him, and the school board tabled the vote.

That was a win for rational thinking over rhetoric, but it was a temporary stay. I admired his integrity and also knew it would usher him out the door. Even though they had seen zero research to back up their lust for those sexy cameras, the community and board members eventually voted to burn the money on them. So for that and other reasons, my colleague resigned at the end of that year and moved up the ranks of school administration in another state. In his new position he has oversight of decisions involving school safety and ensures that comprehensive needs assessments and risk assessments are completed before the district prioritizes resources to promote school safety.

ACCOUNTABILITY > POLICIES

The legal system taps me as an expert witness, and that pays whether my colleagues like me or not. I am one of the leading expert witnesses on safety matters in the country. I'm not a lawyer, so technically you can't say I consistently "win" safety cases, but when I'm brought on board, the scales tip in favor of the firm that retained me. Yes, an expert witness is supposed to be impartial and report to the judge and jury and not the retaining counsel. But because I don't *need* to do any of this, I only accept cases I believe in.

Then I research them until they cry. In a recent case investigating the wrongful death of a student, I pored through about seventeen thousand documents. No, that number is not exaggerated for comic effect. The FedEx trucks would drop off box after box of documents at my house; I'm sure the delivery guy needed time off for herniated discs after that. (He still gives me dirty looks.)

The judge looked at the stack of documentation and shrugged at the defense. The school had failed to handle the pattern of bullying that led to a death, and the proof was before their eyes. *Well, do you guys have anything to say?*

They didn't.

It was my proclivity to digest thousands of documents and recognize the patterns that made it possible to bring individual and systems failures into clear view. Because I had worked on the inside for so long I knew where to look for the flaws; I wasn't thrown off the scent by gingerbread terminology or word salad policies. Not a lot of people have the ability to weave this all together. In the end, the organization trusted in trendy policies and catchphrases instead of doing the hard work of using judgment, discernment, and building positive relationships with students toward impacting their growth and character. It's easy to say, "Spend more," but not as easy to say, "Do your job and take responsibility for it."

So no, I'm not above having anything to lose because of a mysterious shoebox of thumb drives Edward Snowden sent to me. I have nothing to lose because I've spent my entire life building a reputation as a thorough, enthusiastic expert. I don't need to work anymore—but I *am* still working because I love what I do. Perhaps I'll never fully retire, but I like the release it gives me to speak clearly.

I can't be sure, but I think I *am* making schools safer—by carrying out effective drills, training staff, and working with businesses to create student threat reporting systems that are accessible to everyone, including the more than ten million children in the United States that have disabilities such as autism, anxiety, and visual impairments. And armed with the information I have gathered over the years, you have the potential to do the same. I'd like to share that information and just a few stories with you in the coming pages.

If you aren't entirely convinced that bulletproof backpacks are the way to save lives during school shootings, but you can't afford to say anything, this is the book for you: you can at least enjoy nodding along to the text with the silent satisfaction that someone out there gets it. If you are feeling a bit bolder, it might amuse you even more to leave copies of this book in the lounge for people to curiosity read . . . until it slowly catches on.

Acknowledgments

Member Checks

I would like to express my gratitude to the following individuals whose support and insight were invaluable in the development of this book.

Joe Bruzzese
Dr. Seann Dikkers
TJ Martinell
Katie Pechon
Larry Perrodin
Dr. Paul Rapp
Hector Solis
Ann Sterzinger
Mike Valentino
Danny Woodburn

I am indebted to Yvette Clairjeane and the New York City Department of City Planning for being nothing short of wonderful to collaborate with in order to obtain permission to reproduce material owned by the DCP including the map image of Lower Manhattan.

Introduction

School Safety in America

Graphic displays of fake guns, victims with mock wounds, and responders executing a predictive nightmare script are ubiquitous appendages of K–12 school active shooter preparation in the United States. The misplaced focus on rote defensive maneuvers has cash-strapped schools diverting millions of dollars from more effective detection methods to promote a safe school environment.

Regrettably, most school safety preparedness measures are woefully disconnected from what has been revealed by empirical studies on the topic. Research has shown that people behave differently when under pressure, despite their level of preparation, making behaviors difficult if not impossible to predict. Overpreparation can risk distracting from the genuine and more subtle preparation that is needed for situations in which you might be required to do some spontaneous and inventive thinking.

The FBI (U.S. Federal Bureau of Investigation, 2000) notes that most school shooters intentionally or unintentionally revealed clues or indicators sometimes weeks prior to carrying out the attack. This phenomenon is referred to as "leakage," and there are several documented instances in which leakage was detected, acted on, and a potential school shooting was averted.

Yet school fortification has blossomed into an unregulated $3 billion industry resulting in bollards, bulletproof glass, and security cameras. All of these measures haven't altered the trendline of disengaged youth evading fortifications and consistently inflicting harm upon schools. There is a better way.

We must reallocate resources toward leakage detection and away from complicated, sensationalized interagency incident response protocols that are typically irrelevant during an active shooter situation. It's time to fund research into the youth code of silence, teaching youth how to increase their situational awareness skills and revamping our school safety instruction and threat reporting systems to be accessible to the ten million students in America with special needs or language barriers. Imagine moving these youth from the sidelines of safety into important, active roles of monitoring their environments and effectively reporting threats to school safety!

LESSONS FROM LOWER MANHATTAN

This book will use the seemingly impossible but highly successful rescue of half a million people from Lower Manhattan on September 11, 2001, to make a complex argument about the powerful psychological and social forces that must be understood in order to improve school safety.

To boil these ideas down into concrete chunks that you can use on a teaching basis, the book will also use the old "remember these few points and you will have a total system for knowing what to do" trick. The conclusions of this book have been molded into six basic lessons—but there are only four essential pillars of knowledge that you need to carry away.

The first four lessons will be devoted to those four pillars. The last two lessons will consolidate and drive home the proof and reasoning behind the four pillars and then give you an idea of what to expect in the future.

By the time you finish reading, you should know exactly *why* these changes in the profession's outlook need to occur—and you will have a feel for this book's perspective on whether and how change will happen.

To warm you up and give you a taste—and to give you something to refer back to as your curiosity grows—here are the core takeaways from the first four lessons:

1. **The Torus.** The torus is a concept from chaos theory that is easy to understand and fundamental to thinking about the way people see everyday life—and outbreaks of chaos. It is also related to delicious baked goods such as bagels. It contains a crucial corollary: **situational awareness**. Situational awareness is almost important enough for a separate lesson; fortunately for you, it is so simple that it will be rolled into the torus.

2. **The Foolishness of Benchmarking.** Benchmarking is the unfortunate practice of assuming that one occurrence of a type of event, such as a school shooting, is going to unfold just like previous occurrences. Experts assume that you can map one hurricane or forest fire response right onto the next. It is distressingly common among school and

safety professionals, but it ignores the fact that the world is changing all the time.

3. **Drill Fidelity.** You don't need elaborate safety drills. You need solid safety drills.
4. **Systems Will Develop:** People long for security when designing safety systems. But the direct path is not the sure path. Therefore don't plan more than a few minutes into a disaster; it's a waste of time. Instead teach people to go back to following the good natural instincts that the schools have been training them to ignore: creating systems on the fly, identifying the best leaders for the situation, and following them. Instead of planning perfect but fragile systems in advance, prepare people to go with the flow—intelligently.

Each of these lessons will be broken down into succinct chapters to help you understand why the school safety industry needs fundamental change.

Here's what *not* to expect: this isn't a typical book about safety because no one needs another reiteration of any of the conventional (lack of) wisdom. If part of your job is choosing and running safety training for your school, by now you are likely overwhelmed with options, from government and commercial safety experts alike.

Despite the bewildering number of options, however, they are each one size fits all, full of flowcharts, flip charts, and decision trees that tell you exactly what to do if this happens or if that happens, under the assumption that the next crisis will be just like something they've analyzed from a past incident. You can tailor these documents to your school by editing the header. Presto—you've got a safety plan!

But how useful is it to analyze past incidents? In a general sense, knowledge is good, right? But the safety industry seems to get lost in the details every time there's a highly publicized reason to panic.

The 1993 bomb detonation in the basement of the World Trade Center ushered in a robust, redundant array of industry-leading safety measures intended to prevent another bombing of the site. We really went to town under the assumption that the next strike would be similar to the last.

And yet all the reinforced steel barriers, retractable bollards, restricted access, closed streets, security gates, and gun-toting security guards that tens of millions of dollars could buy could not stop the hijacked airliners that finally felled the Twin Towers.

No one saw that one coming, though they went over every inch and microsecond of the previous attempt. But if you search #schoolsafety the first week of September, you'll endlessly scroll endorsements for every school fortification device you could possibly imagine.

Sure, try to fortify your way to safety—but that approach won't work; it never has. Garden variety security breaches of "fortified structures or systems" are a daily occurrence.

Seeing a massively fortified system go down because of the rough equivalent of a box cutter has become so typical that it's part of everyday life. People are constantly notified that their personal data has been compromised by a cybertheft from some retailer, bank, or government agency—often committed by some comically unlikely punk. Most people shake their heads, exhale in disgust, and keep on keeping on.

Novice curiosity seekers with minimal planning manage to foil security at high-profile, well-funded venues fairly regularly. They aren't highly publicized because no one dies, but if a harmless pest can get in, so can a terrorist.

In 2014, for instance, a New Jersey teenager interested in the construction of 1 World Trade Center squeezed through a hole in a fence at Ground Zero in the middle of the night and made his way past several layers of security to the top of the tower. He stayed up for a few hours—taking photos (Garger, Rachmen, & O'Neill, 2016). The sunrise was spectacular.

In 2018, a Pittsburgh Steelers fan outfitted in player equipment commonly sold in stadium pro shops walked past security and onto a National Football League practice field. Fortunately, players (the real ones) recognized the imposter as he tried to participate in team drills (Popejoy, 2018).

This can even happen by accident: late this summer, as per Wisconsin tradition, a family was visiting a Green Bay Packers training camp for fun when they unwittingly wandered into a players-only area. Security quickly hustled the apologetic fans out without incident—but what if they had been angry Vikings fans?

New types of crises are erupting all the time—terrorists and the weather are both becoming quite inventive—and we need to teach staff to respond to new threats on the fly. But instead we are inundating teachers with flowcharts, which sends them a clear signal: the last thing they should rely on is their own good judgment.

The argument of this book—to put it in the terms of the safety profession—is that rote response steps are impractical for nonlinear situations. A school intruder's behavior might match up with the initial steps of a safety plan and then sharply deviate from any sequenced counter-measure. The purpose of this book is to offer a different approach to developing effective responses to crisis situations.

One of the main reasons benchmarking is unreasonable is that there isn't enough data to add up to meaningful statistics. What makes a shooting less likely? We don't have enough numbers for any sane statistician to assure you there is a solid answer.

Although cable news coverage goes nuts over each event that it seems there have been a hundred school shootings a year since the beginning of time, these events are in fact rare. This is a good thing. But it means we don't have a sufficient *n* size—or number of events—to have reasonable confidence in any conclusions.

The FBI has repeatedly stated that there is no such thing as a profile of a school shooter (U.S. Federal Bureau of Investigation, 2000). The best-researched document on what actually decreases school violence is the CDC's Report on School Connectedness (Centers for Disease Control and Prevention, 2009), and nowhere in that document is fortifying a school suggested as a means for decreasing school violence.

But schools want to do something. So they try to benchmark sentinel events—the big news headlines—to their own settings. Fortunately, school shootings are so rare that this approach is statistically senseless. Unfortunately, this means that schools are throwing taxpayers' money at statistical anomalies and pet guesses.

Therefore this book suggests a different approach: use data and ideas from other types of disasters. There may not be enough school shootings to tell you what works, but throw in other incidents, and you've got a slightly clearer picture.

EMBRACE, ASSESS, INVENTORY, DECIDE

If you don't like lists, you can also sum up these recommendations with a mantra: Recognize and embrace that you are in chaos; assess the context and situation; inventory your options; make a decision in the best interest of yourself or those under your care.

Okay, that's pretty long for a mantra.

How about Embrace, Assess, Inventory, and Decide? If you want four words to write on the back of your hand before life throws you a horrible test, there you are.

Embracing chaos might sound flaky, but it is essential to survival. As every suburban school shooting has shown, even the most peaceful life is actually fragile. Anyone might be plunged into chaos at any time, and it's safer to learn to embrace it than to deny it. This book is about safety in a nonlinear world, which is counter-cultural in the safety business. The rote, run-hide-fight stuff that the safety business typically embraces doesn't work anymore, if it ever did.

So Embrace, Assess, Inventory, and Decide. But first, a preliminary lesson on what *not* to do.

PRELIMINARY LESSON: YOU CAN'T FORTIFY YOUR WAY TO SAFETY (AND OTHER BAD IDEAS YOU'VE BEEN SOLD)

Fortifications feel safe. At some point in evolution, our distant ancestors were tiny mammals burrowing away from the dinosaurs, and we still like that walled-in feeling. But it's often an illusory comfort, especially when our walls encounter things we didn't think of when we built them.

For example, France was convinced that it could fortify its way to safety by constructing the impressive Maginot Line in the 1930s. Unfortunately, the Germans just went around it, marching through Belgium, and the French countryside was quickly overrun by German military forces at the beginning of World War II.

The Maginot Line has since become a metaphor for expensive efforts that offer a false sense of security. Many people market their services in this field, but those who employ them are often unaware that there is not actually a standardized certification for being a "safety professional." And many of these uncertified professionals are selling schools some very, very expensive Maginot Lines.

To put it bluntly, safety pros have taken that mammalian instinct to put one's back against the wall and used it to milk school districts for hundreds of thousands of dollars' worth of fixes that often do more harm than good.

SCHOOL SAFETY: THE BILLION DOLLAR INDUSTRY

Safety has become a multibillion-dollar industry in the years since 9/11 (Ma, 2018), so there is much incentive to market safety gear. That is why, for example, you will hear claims that a particular and incredibly expensive camera system (coincidentally, it's the one they're selling) can give you magic safety, regardless of any other conditions that affect the situation that day.

Likewise, many school officials and parents unthinkingly accept the idea that metal detectors are a worthwhile expense. Sure, why not? Don't let anybody just waltz into the school carrying a gun, right? It sounds fine at first glance—well, it sounds fine to a layperson who refuses to listen to me when I tell them over and over again the fundamental uselessness of metal detectors that safety expert Kenneth Trump has also been trying to drive home for years.

Take Luke Woodham, the Pearl, Mississippi, shooter. Luke told Secret Service agents that if he'd been faced with a metal detector, he would have "walked right through it" (Dedman, 2006). Officials at Columbine High School concluded that metal detectors would not have thwarted that attack either.

Why don't they work? Simple. The only way for a metal detector to do you any good is if you can (a) have one at every door, (b) staff it at any possible hour that people might be going in and out of the building, and (c) seal all the windows closed forever (Trump, 2015).

And nobody would think to sneak in a gun through the propped gym door behind the dumpsters where the kids go to smoke, right? They don't ever look at those doors and realize they could smuggle in contraband as they're sneaking out to cut class. Nah, kids who plan to be armed in school always take their guns through the four main entrances between the hours of 8:00 a.m. and 3:00 p.m.

So on *this* planet metal detectors bring exactly one benefit: ten minutes of quiet from the screeching chorus of worried parents.

A BETTER IDEA: ASK YOUR INSURANCE COMPANY

You've still got those distressed parents, though . . . they want action. (Perhaps a lot of action, depending on how deep their pockets are.) How do you spend the money the right way?

Here's an idea that has worked in many districts. Replace those unregulated "experts" with people who have a financial reason to want a school to stay safe, plus loads of experience: *Go to the school's liability insurance carrier, and ask them to send inspectors.*

Yep, the insurance company. Everybody hates them, but who else knows risks like they do?

These insurance company inspectors examine hundreds of schools a year, they have an incentive to distinguish genuine threats from nonthreats, and best of all, they aren't marketing anything. Their financial interest lies with your interests: they want your school to be safe so they don't have to pay out after a disaster. A safety expert, on the other hand, wants to make a commission.

A lot of schools don't think to do this, or else they're afraid that if the assessor finds problems, they'll be faced with expensive fixes, a higher insurance premium, or even that they'll lose their coverage.

But this isn't a problem most of the time. Even if the assessors find fixes, they are genuine, may save lives, and nine times out of ten they are cheaper than what the safety pro is going to sell to you. (If you think you're going to let a safety pro walk onto your campus without spending money, then you're the guy in the horror movie who thinks it's okay to ask a vampire into the house.)

Many principals feel that the safety pro is "their guy" and that the insurance company inspector is on the enemy team, going to bat for the insurance company. But this is just a feeling . . . the kind of feels that professional salespeople are great at making you feel. That's their job, remember?

The insurance company assessor, on the other hand, may not seem like such a chummy guy or gal. That's because he or she is too busy looking for genuine risks to pretend to be your new best friend.

Also, the insurance company's assessor is more likely to have access to geographic information system (GIS) mapping software that can import, analyze, and display social data sets, such as crime statistics, that can be overlaid to the specific location of your school.

Ever wonder why people of similar age and driving records pay significantly different premiums for insuring the same make and model of vehicle? GIS algorithms factor in crime, weather, wildlife populations, and so on to generate the risk per vehicle per location. GIS provides information that objectively helps inform the school of a comprehensive inventory of risks, from crime to severe weather.

All this info can pinpoint risks that schools frequently overlook. For example, from the social vulnerability map included in the School Security and Crisis Preparedness presentation on Wisconsin Public Television (Perrodin, 2013), you can track binge drinking, tornado touchdowns, and locations of nuclear power plants across every county in the state. Hey, if the data reveal that you're living in a tornado alley, then perhaps you should conduct more tornado drills—especially if everyone's going to be tipsy. (Oh, and look out for the tornado running into the nukes.)

You won't get this from your vendor. If you're lucky, she might understand most of her sales script. But she is not informed, nor does she care, about the data-stacked hierarchy of risks for the specific school. She will use fear to talk you into all kinds of cool, overpriced turrets and towers to snap onto the school building. It's teaching inside of a LEGO® set—and about as safe!

Imagine donning a snazzy knit hat (complete with tassel) that supposedly accommodates any noggin. Yes, it looks fabulous, but whether you're happy you chose it once you're stuck outside in it depends on what month it is and where you are.

Say it's a light, stylish hat, meant for March treks in Rhode Island. The boutiques in Warwick and Woonsocket can't keep them in stock! It's miserable in North Dakota's subzero winters, but a safety vendor would bring a box to Fargo in February anyway. Vendors ignore context; they push you to mold the school to the device or system and not the other way around.

So why do school boards hire these clowns? Because they can control what their private contractor does with the report. They end up wearing a beanie to Antarctica, but at least the parents don't learn about any of their screw-ups.

This is how they deal with selling you equipment. When they sell you drills, it's even worse: mix a million flip charts and flowcharts with a theater production, complete with fake blood. Is that a good use of your resources or just a dead horse they're beating on because kids have been doing fire drills for a hundred years? Disasters are by definition unpredictable, chaotic, and dynamic. You don't need complex drills. It's impossible to rehearse the specifics. You need to teach people a new way of engaging with their surroundings.

THE BENCHMARKING PARADOX

Clever readers may notice that although benchmarking specific policies to mimic the past is a sketchy practice, many of the observations in this book are based on past events. The past is useful, but there isn't enough school data to dictate present or future best practices; even if there were, the past will never cleanly replicate. This is why teaching flexibility is as important as understanding 9/11 or any other disaster.

And yet this text will keep returning to the improbable evacuation of Lower Manhattan on September 11, 2001—partly because one of the lessons of Lower Manhattan was precisely that: you never know what's coming.

That's what disasters like 9/11 can teach you: over and over, they have shown that they have nothing too specific to teach you. What they *can* teach you is a general approach, one you must internalize and share.

September 11, 2001, was a shining example of why the best laid plans of mice and men are often tossed aside for some better stuff born of improvisation.

As wave after wave of chaos unfolded, somehow five hundred thousand people were herded to Battery Park, where they found an impromptu fleet of hundreds of rescue boats that took them to safety in around nine hours.

That is the historical fact. How did it happen?

Do you remember public officials running drills with fishing boats carrying everyone in Manhattan to New Jersey every fifth Tuesday during the school year? Nah. Heck, nobody even practiced going to the park.

THE RESCUE: SUNNY SKIES AND ADMIRAL LOY

New York Harbor is a precarious body of water to navigate on a good day because it is a commercial/recreation mixed-use harbor. There are large vessels, ferries crossing, big wakes, and heavy traffic areas, as well as tiny human-powered vessels.

And weather can make or break a boating experience in the harbor. It is routinely altered by winds, waves, fog, sheeting rain, strong currents, tidal height changes between three feet and eight feet, blizzard whiteouts, and ice. Boat captains share harrowing tales of near collisions, rough seas, and mechanical failures, honing their situational awareness as a barber straightens a blade along a leather strop.

Daybreak on September 11, 2001, rewarded captains with a favorable weather forecast. Winds were calm at nine miles per hour, the air temperature was 81 degrees Fahrenheit, and it was mostly sunny; visibility was ten miles and the sunset was at 7:13 p.m. It was a perfect day for the largest boat rescue in history (Wunderground, 2001).

The key to understanding that improbable rescue is not just understanding the conditions, although everything from the weather to the day of the week was incredibly lucky. One 9/11 compilation video on YouTube begins with an ironic collection of clips featuring local newscasters on the September 11, 2001, morning news, crowing about what a beautiful, perfect September day they were having in New York, forty minutes or so before the first plane hit the towers and the Furies broke loose. (One newscaster even said: "It's too quiet.")

The lesson also lies in the expectations and life experiences of the people who were rescued. What did they expect in a disaster? What were they looking for? Why didn't they trample each other running for the boats? What went right about human nature that day?

The boats appeared because they answered a call from U.S. Coast Guard Admiral James Loy. Admiral Loy was interviewed for the eleven-minute documentary *Boatlift* (Rosenstein, 2011), where he cut an impressive figure of emerging leadership in a crisis, skilled with both improvisation and delegation as well as knowing New York Harbor.

Admiral Loy had no protocols or flowcharts. Nor did he send his make-shift fleet a detailed set of instructions. He got on the designated Marine Radio emergency channel, a means of communication that all boaters in the harbor would have known to turn to for general announcements in an emergency. He called out for anyone with a boat to assess the situation and do whatever they could safely do to rescue people. He created a nearly perfect case study in what the profession calls "distributed leadership." Which is what it sounds like: distributing leadership responsibilities over as many independent unit leaders as the situation requires.

INSTITUTIONAL MEMORY AND PROJECTED BENCHMARKING

Leadership *had* to be distributed: no one person knew how every responding vessel would function within a developing system. This points up another crucial element of safety that professionals too often miss: the importance of institutional memory.

Many school principals these days last no more than one or two years; we hand them a five-pound ring of keys, and they'll leave before they know what more than ten of those keys are for. They know they will be burned out or transferred in a year or two, so why bother learning?

This results in a lack of institutional knowledge that drastically impairs people's ability to help build a rescue system in a crisis. The deeper the knowledge base, the more solutions people can devise.

Fortunately, this institutional memory was present on 9/11; re-creating it in our school systems will take deep change. Staff need to feel they have a stake in knowing the institution where they work. This means developing a solid induction process that includes updated training videos and mentors to account for the nonstop turnover of school leaders and teachers and the ever-growing number of transient families.

Experts instead focus on assembling advisory groups, including parents, to "give everyone a voice" in school safety. Ugh. This appeals to school leaders, as it gives the illusion of collaboration and it diffuses responsibility for future decisions: if you really mess up, blame the group—a group dominated by nonexperts. Give them a voice—that sounds nice!—and then when everything blows up, gee, that's what they asked for!

Do you bring in local astronomers and dog walkers to choose your next firetruck? No, but for some reason they do it with school safety. These groups' main function is to create "safety by consensus" flip charts to tack beside the classroom door. Good luck figuring out where they've alphabetized "I can't count how many shooters there are" when there are bullets whizzing past your ears.

Even more money is spent on "projected benchmarking," the attitude that "if it happened somewhere, then it could happen here, so we had better start panicking and buying shiny surveillance cameras in advance."

Projected benchmarking is also great for local news media who need to fill air time. Headline: "It could happen here, so let's pretend it did and get everyone in a frenzy instead of writing a real news story."

School shootings make lazy newscasters' lives nationwide very easy for the next few days. Local stations hundreds of miles from a school shooting wag microphones at school officials and police, who should wisely decline to comment until the investigation of the event has been completed.

Nope! Instead they've invented a subgenre of "projected benchmarking": the even stupider idea that "it *could* have happened here, but it didn't, because we bought these awesome bulletproof window coatings."

Ironically, they usually get their scant knowledge of what happened from the clickbait mass media coverage, so these interviews are just an endless, tail-biting snake of clueless media using school officials to talk through another.

After both the Sandy Hook and the September 11, 2001, attacks, the media went school to school asking, "What would you do if this happened here?" An amazing number of schools felt compelled to spill their district's intricate safety response protocols and blueprint-grade maps of school buildings to parents and local media in an attempt to assure panicked parents of their preparedness. Yeesh. Look: You don't share your battle plans with anyone.

And school safety is an ongoing, never-ending process. You shouldn't be jolted to action because of September 11, 2001. What were you doing on September 10, 2001? Telling the terrorists' moms exactly where your security cameras were?

On the other hand, after both of these tragedies, many schools provided parents with advice on how to talk to their child about high-profile acts of violence, which is in fact helpful—not in stopping attackers, but in helping kids make sense of it all. Schools can serve as a clearinghouse for helping parents with strategies to reassure children that they are safe.

But why spill your detailed safety plans to nerve-racked parents? Then they ramp up the drills and form advisory groups and listening sessions. This means letting parents sit in auditoriums after work, giving themselves sleep deprivation, and taking up their downtime to talk about how worried they are and recite school safety recommendations they heard about on the news.

Though useless, these worry-ins present an opportunity to be a victim and a blame thrower, which is why they remain popular.

What we learned from September 11, 2001, is that it takes about two weeks for things to return to normal on a broad level. On September 24, 2001, the National Football League and many other sports leagues began returning to their regular schedules; at a time when the country was still filled with angst and gloom, the Packers and Redskins gave the American people a much-needed taste of solace and normalcy.

It's not callous to move on, nor is it crazy to freak out at first; it's life. Either we process chaos and move on or chaos burns itself out—or we simply recalibrate to a "new" normal that is out in the land of chaos.

The gravity of similarity will bring you back to Earth. For example, one fellow out in the Midwest had an electrical power substation abutting his property. Hours after the September 11, 2001, attacks, per self-appointment, he was standing guard at the power station—rifle in hand. Sounds extreme, right? Yeah, but he was doing what he felt he had to do, and a day later he wasn't standing out there anymore.

Back in 2001, even though many of the rescuers in the harbor were amateur, there was a great deal of institutional memory all around, even spread throughout the lay population. This mix of ingredients resulted in a highly coordinated response with no advance planning . . . well, no *specific* advance planning.

As this book will show you, in a chaotic situation, systems will develop as people gravitate toward leadership positions. The key is not to tell them exactly how to assemble themselves but to prepare people to have the mental acuity in a crisis to take part in the system's development.

If you had hundreds of captains awaiting directives before they could chug ahead a few boat lengths, the rescue would have never come together. It would be like a bad day at the McDonald's® drive-thru window.

Moreover, if all of those captains had been employed in Boston Harbor until two weeks ago, and nobody had given them any training about New York, then it also might not have come together either.

As Loy said in *Boatlift*, "The real reality after I put out some direction was in the hands of commanders and captains who were the respective captains of the port and did what they needed to do, including all the stuff I told them to do and whatever else they felt was appropriate" (Rosenstein, 2011).

Such loose directives, especially in the context of the unprecedented chaos following the attack on the World Trade Center, seem like a guaranteed prescription for monumental failure—and yet the evacuation was accomplished without injuries or fatalities.

The Manhattan rescue didn't come from a flip chart. Rather, the seeds for this response were sown in the participants' educations and their experiences. This is a main reason why we cannot draw one-to-one "how-to" lessons from the Manhattan evacuation: the generation that was evacuated on September 11 grew up in a very different world.

A lot of the difference is clearly related to the rise of social media use and the corresponding shift away from "meat-world" social reality and personal responsibility.

Current students (a) post their fears openly on social media and call for change, although they don't really know what "change" is, and (b) adore walkouts and protests.

They also are convinced guns are the problem; conveniently, legislators can be pestered into fixing it for them. Change doesn't come from within; they confuse helping themselves with demanding stuff from authorities. Older generations didn't wait for help, they made it. Now everyone, including the older generations, is being sucked into the temptation to demand that the Internet or somebody on high figure everything out for them. But what if there's no time to consult the authorities? What if the Internet goes out?

So the lessons we draw from September 11 for school safety must be more general and philosophical than we might like. Most educators and safety professionals are used to working with very specific step-by-step instructions. As modern Americans—or simply as human beings—we really like straightforward directions.

This desire is natural. But in a disaster, it's counterproductive. What's more useful? Well, baked goods are a good place to start.

Part I

The Torus

Chapter One

How Thinking about a Bagel Can Get You through the Worst Day of Your Life

You might not give your morning bagel much thought. Bagels are delicious. And thanks to the American flair for cherry picking the most convenient and tasty foods from every culture and working them into our everyday grub vocabulary, this once distinctively Jewish food is now conveniently available everywhere.

They're not particularly nutritious, unless you count the cream cheese, but bagels are food for thought. They're round breads, a never-ending tube with a hole in the center. This shape is good for sticking a hook through so you can dip them in boiling water, the traditional way to craft a good bagel. But that simple shape is also shared by our best visual approximations of some bleeding-edge scientific concepts.

In fact, this isn't the first book that uses bagels to explain something that seems hard to describe. The physicist, rock publicist, philosopher, and writer Howard Bloom used the shape of a bagel way back in the mid-twentieth century to come up with a hypothesis to explain his most difficult ideas about quantum physics, decades before the larger scientific community decided that his ideas were right (Bloom, 2012).

The bagel shape seems to be a good engine of pareidolia, a fifty-cent vocabulary word we'll get into later. (As it turns out, there is very little in the universe that can't be explained with bakery treats.)

Luckily, although this book will touch on a bit of chaos theory—don't worry, it's kind of fun—we are not going to plunge readers quite so deep into the minds of the gods as a quantum physician, and there will be no math.

But the topic might be more interesting than the fundamental properties of time and space, or at least it will hit closer to home: our bagel is about human nature, and the way everyone—including the students we want to protect—moves through the world.

We're going to talk about something social scientists unhelpfully call a "torus." This is a daunting word to throw out there. "Torus" sounds like Latin, but it's actually a fake Latin word somebody made up in the 1500s.

We need students to directly engage with the idea of the bagel, but when most people hear words like this, they tune out. Suddenly everything sounds like Charlie Brown's teacher talking—*wa wa wa*—but the experts go on torus-ing furiously anyway.

This is a bad thing because the torus bagel—*not* escape paths, *not* duck and cover drills—is one of the most important things you need to teach your students about keeping them safe.

They need to understand what a torus is. But don't just teach them the vocabulary word. Teach them the fundamental meaning of the torus and how it relates to their safety.

Here are the basics. A torus (our bagel) is a way of visualizing the cloud of familiar places, events, and daily routines that people are accustomed to— and the interruptions to those daily routines.

Our day-to-day is kind of a cloud but also kind of a circle. As people go through their life routines, doing things and going places that are familiar to them, they are said to be "within their torus."

We visualize this torus as a bagel-shaped ring. We move about within it, going roughly in a circle, making one revolution around the torus, more or less, every twenty-four hours.

Our home and work and daily routine are at the center of the dough tube, surrounded by our most familiar neighborhoods. Things we do fairly often, streets we walk on once in a while, are a bit further out, actions we know about but might have never done and side streets we have possibly never seen but that are related to our inner world are out on the crust.

The streets grow less and less familiar, the actions more and more dimly related to your daily experience, as they approach the crust. Approaching the crust of the bagel is akin to venturing into a neighborhood in your city where you have never been. Outside the crust . . . is Albuquerque. (Unless you've been to Albuquerque.)

Time moves you along the tube as you perform your daily revolution; experiences and places move you toward the crust of the bagel, as you move from the familiar to the less familiar and toward the space around the torus, which is not familiar at all. So we visualize the torus as a bagel-shaped field of experiences and places.

We can also visualize the countless events, places, and people we *could* be experiencing as a vast bakery, inside of which our bagel is situated. The bakery is large, and it is inside of a shopping district, and the district is inside of a city . . . but we live most of our lives going around and around inside of that bagel, like a molecule of flour.

Despite the nearly infinite combinations of possible activities we could be carrying out and all the places we could go on this Earth, the activities and experiences of most human beings all usually remain within the bagel.

In fact, we have spent so much time inside of this bagel that we don't even know much about the bagels sitting in the next basket—never mind knowing where the cash register is, even though we have heard it might be out there.

Some of us occasionally jump on an airplane and, metaphorically speaking, find ourselves in the magical new world of the store up the street; however, if we travel often, then the experience of travel itself can become situated inside of our bagel. (Remember, the bagel is not really representative of physical space, it is a metaphor for our personal world as our mind sees it.)

Further, most people, most of the time, are to be found near the center of the tube of bread—deep inside the bagel, perhaps unaware that someone is currently beginning to bite into its crust.

This is partly because most people are required to keep to something of a strict routine in order to remain employed or to finish school. We move tightly through the commute-study-work-home bit of the bagel, perhaps with variations such as picking up an actual bagel at Starbucks® in the morning rather than our usual Dunkin Donuts®, and maybe going out once or twice a week at night—but then tomorrow morning, 8:00 a.m., obligation requires us to be sucked back into the center of the tube.

However, there is another reason most people more or less agree to this arrangement, a psychological one: Humans find comfort in regularity.

We may tire of the office routine, but when we go on that longed-for vacation, the first thing we do when we arrive in a country far outside our torus is to make a base camp at the hotel. Then we don't feel quite right until we stake out which bars and restaurants we shall commute to on a more or less daily basis.

We overfill our suitcases with familiar things before we go—this is why you pack fourteen shirts for a seven-day trip even though you know it's silly—and we cannot wait to shake the exhausting disruption of air travel so we can fall into a daily rhythm of sightseeing and dining. Congratulations, you have just created a new lump on the bagel—it just happens to be in Spain. (It is very seldom that we are genuinely out of our bagel. In fact, when it becomes impossible to remain inside of the torus, it is usually because the system around us has been thrown into a state of chaos.)

We *like* being inside the bagel, and though these adventures may be fun, we get very tired after a while and want to retire back deep inside, where we cannot sniff the crust.

Very few thrill-seeking and curious types really savor being out on the crust for long, much less outside of it. However, outside of that crust is where we are suddenly thrust when a disaster strikes—and we don't get to argue about it.

If we try to negotiate with reality to get back into the bagel, in fact, we usually wind up as casualties.

Unfortunately, the panic of a disaster can cause people to try harder than usual to cling to normalcy.

In the early twentieth century, there was a series of deadly fires in movie houses. People trapped in those dark infernos would stubbornly try to exit the building the same way they entered it, no matter how far they were from their original entry door.

Even if they were near another exit, they kept running for that familiar door—it is part of their torus, which they are desperately trying to remain inside. As a consequence, many people died in the lobbies after running past *marked exits.* They were unfamiliar with chaos and so instinctively tried to return to the comforts of a state of normalcy that had been blown apart.

Unfortunately, denying the reality of chaos is the riskiest thing you can do.

And this is why you need to teach your students about the bagel and try as hard as you can to get them to poke their noses outside of it once in a while.

Although practically no one likes being rudely thrust outside of the torus, disasters are going to do it whether we like it or not, so we had better be prepared—not just by knowing where the exits to the school auditorium are located but by knowing how it feels to be outside of the torus and how to keep a level head despite that discomfort.

Otherwise, we just run for the door we came in. Bagels are made to be thrust between someone's teeth. Students who try to crawl back in may be swallowed.

"Teaching the torus"—explaining this bakery item to students and then finding ways to get them to explore outside of it—is one of the most fundamental steps to improving school safety. But asking people to head for the crust and explore when they don't have to goes against our paradoxical nature as human beings.

Remember: You can voluntarily leave your bagel. But if you are thrown out of it—or if the bagel itself becomes severed—it is because of a chaotic situation.

Both of these ways of being outside the bagel are uncomfortable. But if you *choose* to leave it before you're forced out, you get to practice coping with that uncomfortable feeling on your own terms. Otherwise, if your first time out of the bagel is a festival of surprises, now you have the discomfort *and* the disaster to learn to deal with all at once.

REALITY AND RESPONSIBILITIES

Thus, it is extremely important to teach this idea to your students and to teach them that they need to practice venturing outside the bagel.

People expect similarity in our lives and strive for sameness—even though sameness is mathematically impossible. No two items or activities can ever be identical in composition or occupy the same space in a given point in time. Even the most precise efforts will only ever result in similar outcomes.

In manufacturing, this is known as "acceptable tolerances." A demonstration of acceptable tolerances is the Hoover Dam, an engineering marvel . . . that leaks. This isn't a cause for concern, as designers of the dam were fully aware that the most exacting precision in building the structure couldn't account for the trickles of water that would seep through, around, or under the gigantic block of concrete.

Structures and systems (which include humans) will have inherent variations that don't really affect their intended purpose. Many believe we can remove such "tolerances" from safety. We can't, so we must adapt to them and manage them accordingly.

No matter how many commercials you see featuring a parent weeping because his or her son or daughter would still be alive if the school had bought Security Camera Brand Z, don't be fooled.

These commercials prey on our tendency to confuse similarity for sameness. Imagine laying a dozen 1973 pennies on a table. You study the coins and note the scuffs and patina unique to each. Yet if asked if the pennies were all the same, most of us would say, sure. They're all worth one cent. All discs stamped with a picture of Abe Lincoln. But in their physical details they are all different and at no point in time were they ever the same.

Such can be said for every day—and for each of us. We aren't even identical to ourselves. We are both material and spiritual beings, influenced by instincts and archetypes, and we change ever so slightly with every breath and exhalation—and much more with an infusion of adrenaline to our circulatory system. We change as we learn and experience things; it instills in us both bias and expectations.

Well, maybe some of us stop learning at around age forty. School principals, for instance, notoriously plow forward with absurd decisions, then use them as a precedent for even more absurd decisions.

This is a true story: one principal purchased a baseball bat for every classroom so they could fight off possible intruders, presumably because back when he was a kid that would have been effective.

There is nothing wrong with having biases and expectations based on our experience, any more than there is something wrong with getting hungry after a long walk; we're people and that's what happens to us.

But when we are entrusted with the safety of students, we have a duty to be self-aware about our biases and expectations so that we will base school safety decisions on the available research and our awareness of human behavior in a crisis.

When we are in our personal torus, change slowly and inevitably happens around us, even if it eludes our daily notice. However, days that are consecutive are similar, and most trends in the future can be forecast to some degree—when the bagel is intact, that is.

Different processes can also be described as forming their own torus inside of the daily torus, the way the day's bagel loops within the bagel of an ordinary year.

Bagels inside of bagels inside of bagels, man!

Sounds almost . . . cosmically delicious. What could possibly go wrong?

The morning of Tuesday, September 11, 2001, the typical Twin Towers worker began the day with a crowded commute, coffee, traveling to a floor in a multistory office building, booting up a computer, and perhaps chatting by the copier about the previous night's Thirtieth Anniversary Celebration show at Madison Square Garden and the dazzling wardrobe selections that Michael Jackson and Elizabeth Taylor chose for the event.

In other words, they were deep in their torus.

When something is within its torus, we can say that it is predictable and will produce a stable "outcome basin"—a set of reasonably likely outcomes.

For example, in the 9/11 scenario, the expected outcome basin for your trip to work would center on arriving at work that morning one way or another, with minor variations. If you are used to getting to your office in the Twin Towers by 9:00 a.m. but today you arrive at 9:10, that means your trip to work today is not identical to yesterday's, but both have fallen within the range of a stable outcome basin.

And like Pavlov's dogs, we expect to find roughly what we usually find at work and begin to anticipate those experiences.

If you are used to getting to your office in the Twin Towers by noon and they are gone . . . well, you're out of your bagel. (So stop drooling over whatever you're used to eating at your desk and get ready to run.)

Normally, expecting a stable outcome basin is helpful: it saves us the mental energy we would waste if we always ran every cue from the environment through our conscious mind. People are hardwired to fall into energy-saving modes, which is why it is so difficult to snap out of it when chaos hits.

We are adept at convincing ourselves that things will "return to normal." If the subway car stops in the tunnel, it will start again in a minute or two, as it typically has in the past. (By the time we admit that the train is on fire and we should try to escape into the tunnel, we are beginning to suffocate.)

The blizzard will stall the city for a day or two, but the snow will be shoveled from sidewalks and scooped from roads. We've been through this before. We know what to expect. Until . . . oh, jeez, there's a building missing.

So the bagel is a snack we can count on, until it isn't—and the further from it we are, the more of a chaotic state we're in.

While this may not be our first choice of places to hang out, there's one upside: decisions become simpler to make in direct correlation to the amount of chaos in the system.

On an ordinary day in the grocery store, you have a dizzying array of products and brands from which to choose. If there is a food shortage due to a catastrophe, on the other hand, and most of the shelves are empty, your decision is easy: rice or bread?

If the grocery store is collapsing thanks to an earthquake and there's only one usable exit, it's simpler still. The trick is to realize that you're in a chaos situation as soon as possible, quit thinking about which flavor of Pop-Tarts® sounds good, and run for that door. (The closest door, not the one you came in!)

This is why "teaching the bagel" is so important, and not just as a concept; we actually have to create outside-the-bagel experiences for ourselves and our students if we hope to survive a disaster.

To be prepared, we need to become familiar with the uncomfortable sensation of being outside of the torus. Somewhat ironically, though, if we venture outside of the torus often enough, being outside of the bagel begins to actually become part of the bagel.

Just as someone who travels often begins to experience travel as "someplace I go often," if we venture outside of the bagel enough, we will begin to feel that chaos is something of a familiar place—and we will know how to function inside of it.

Those World Trade Center workers who were "tuned in" to knowing the coordinates of self relative to bagel were able to respond quicker and more decisively to preserve their own safety. They almost instantly transitioned from "Whoa" to "Something's wrong with the bagel—I need to get myself to a safe place."

Those who got stuck on "Whoa" or reverted to "Well, I'm sure it will be fine" did not do so well.

But how do we train students to think outside the bagel—short of throwing them into a burning building? We can start, perhaps, with talking to focus groups of six or eight students at a time about it rather than just tossing surveys at them.

We could also start by talking the school board and parents out of canceling perfectly reasonable field trips.

A recent scandal—or what should have been a scandal, anyway—showcases an instance in which teachers and parents had a perfect chance to give kids a mild dose of life outside their torus . . . and instead they shut them in as tightly as they could.

It might *feel* like it's safe to lock your kids up and swallow the key. But that only makes their bagel smaller. Which makes way too much of the world look like a disaster to them. You can't function as an adult with a mini bagel.

The next chapter will tell you way more about mini bageling than you ever wanted to know. But you should read it anyway . . . because it's also about why it's so important to stretch our safety zones.

Chapter Two

Exploration Is a Kind of Safety Drill

Imagine you're in the eighth grade. You're curious, excited, and ready for bonding experiences with your peers and adventures outside your comfort zone—even if all the adults around you seem to think the world out there is nothing but terrorists and poisoned bottles of Tylenol. (We may make fun of millennials, but 1980s babies will never be capable of taking a pill that isn't safety wrapped.)

Although some of the grown-ups' neurotic fears have begun to infect you, the adolescent hormones that have nudged kids out of their bagels since time immemorial are still managing to flash you another message: *You need to learn about this amazing world.*

However, you live in a small town where the main excitement is volleyball practice and cow tipping.

True, your parents' house is near a forest preserve with hundreds of acres of woodland stretching magically in all directions; when he was your age, your dad spent weekends exploring it.

However, when a girl got trapped under a falling log there fifteen years ago, the local authorities called in a safety expert to assess the situation. He recommended that parents be slapped with neglect charges if they allow kids to go in alone.

You are allowed to go on the playground, but it's not what it once was. When you were a toddler, there was a giant play structure made of whole logs of pine in the local park; it was as tall as a two-story house, and you couldn't wait to get big enough to play on it.

But just as you got tall enough, they razed and replaced it with a prefab maze, two feet off the ground and plastered with safety instructions.

So you and your friends seek excitement the only way you can: playing video games from the couch. You get an adrenaline rush, but you know there is no actual danger. You're sitting inside of your bagel mainlining stress hormones.

However, there's a light at the end of the tunnel. Your class has an exciting trip to Washington, DC, scheduled!

Okay, it isn't New York or Paris, but it is the capital of your country and larger than your current torus to an almost unimaginable degree—your imagination fires around the idea of this trip.

As a normal human adolescent, the prospect of exploring, even in a chaperoned herd, is delicious in a way you don't quite understand.

It's the most exciting thing that has ever happened in your life, including your first kiss—assuming you were ever left unchaperoned with another adolescent.

You've been starving for this. They might even convince you to enjoy the museums . . .

Aaaaaaand then somebody decides it's too much.

Before you even know what hit you, you and your friends' parents have canceled the entire experience.

Their heads are still full of 9/11 and other scares and disasters. There are statistics that could tell them that the kids are more likely to be killed by lightning at home than at every point on the DC trip put together, including touring the White House, but your well-meaning parents have convinced each other and the school that it is too dangerous for thirteen-year-olds with chaperones to tour national monuments during the daytime.

In the blink of an eye, you're stuck at home with no parole . . . again.

How would that feel? I would feel like I was being robbed. These kids had every right to be beside themselves. [1]

But being angry and upset is a student's best-case scenario in this situation. The worst-case scenario is that this type of aggressive helicoptering gives you fears and neuroses that can dictate your behavior for years to come.

These helicopter parents didn't just steal that experience; they probably talked the kids into believing that it was for the best.

This betrayal runs deep. Between cutting their kids' exploration opportunities off at the knees and robbing them of a treat in the name of "your own good," these parents are complicit in a psychological concept called the youth code of silence.

When kids feel they don't have input in the decisions that impact them, they disconnect from "the system." Initiative hasn't gotten them anywhere. Excitement has been followed by more cruel boredom. So they slouch into the path of least resistance.

This is dangerous. We want youth to come forward and report threats to adults, but they won't do it if they already feel marginalized. Passive kids who let you strap them into a car seat at age twelve are not safe (no matter how much they silently hate you).

In the end, these kids were offered a virtual field trip to DC in place of the coveted real trip, complete with digital images of the real artifacts at the Smithsonian. They could look that up online; further, the students aren't learning to deal with being in a new environment—no more than they are learning to deal with combat stress when they play video games.

A major difference between the people who were rescued on 9/11 and the people you must rescue in school shootings now is that the average 9/11 rescuee had a comparatively huge torus. Sure, the average rescuee was forty years old and had spent far more time on this Earth; but they grew up on a different Earth.

Thanks to increasing restrictions on what parents are allowed to let kids do for themselves, kids' toruses are comically tiny. Today, Tom Sawyer's parents would be tossed in jail for neglect. This is not a joke; parents are getting arrested for letting their twelve year olds walk to the park. As recently as the 1980s, ten-year-old girls were hired as babysitters. Now the same age group that used to be qualified for the job of mom #2 needs mom #1 by their side just to cross the street.

But most parents are on board. According to Google's statistics on word use, the term "helicopter parent" appears to have been coined in 1985. It puttered along until about 2002, then shot into fairly common usage and has been increasing in use ever since. Anxious parents, guilt-tripped by the twenty-four-hour news cycle and the Great Recession, respond with blankies and opium tea to their sixteen-year-olds' every anxiety, even calling their children's college professors to complain about their grades.

David Derbyshire interviewed members from four generations of a family to understand the loss of unsupervised outdoors freedom over the span of eight decades. From what they shared with him, he created a disturbing land map showing the collapse of the "roaming range" afforded to children in a single family, arguing it represented a general trend (Derbyshire, 2007).

A century back, children (age eight) were allowed to explore a thirty-square-mile region surrounding their home. Now? The average kid's "roam zone" is one. One square mile. That is a maximum of just over a half-mile from the home in any direction. That's not a bagel; it's a Froot Loop®.

Safety is a paradoxical science: the harder you try to shelter kids from all chaos, the more vulnerable you make them to the inevitable weirdness of life.

Yet you can't go too far in the other direction. Ironically, when it comes to doing *specific* drills—simulating shooter situations that have already happened in other schools—school districts love to scare the heck out of the staff and the students with unnecessarily realistic terror tactics. These inflict what is called "drill trauma," which has already led to lawsuits.

Stay the course! "Teaching the torus" doesn't mean throwing kids into situations in which they can be killed or traumatized. It means allowing them to slowly grow up. The risk of students dying on a field trip to the capital is minuscule—but the benefit gained from traveling to the nation's capital, both in terms of learning about the world and mastering new environments, would have been immense.

As safety professionals, we must work to preserve the authentic torus. If not, we'll have dodo bird kids for the next generation: they'll be wiped out by any adversity as their tiny, fragile torus shatters at the first breath of icy wind.

What can we do? First, get out ahead of panicked parents with real stats and information before they cancel kids' growth experiences. Better yet, get the concept of the bagel into parents' and students' heads.

TJ Martinell, an accomplished writer at the Tenth Amendment Center, was a guest on The Safety Doc Podcast shortly after this DC debacle. He urged dissenters in such communities to remember the Tenth Amendment, a constitutional right that guarantees our ability to take over if the government fails. If they drop the ball, we can push them aside. (Keep this in mind; a later chapter examines grassroots rescue forces that were able to spring up under the auspices of the Tenth Amendment.)

Martinell reminds us that risk was at the center of founding the United States. The irony is obvious. The Founding Fathers embraced unfathomable peril, and 242 years later their heirs won't let kids be herded into the Smithsonian to see the muskets.

"When the Declaration of Independence was signed, these men were likely signing their own death warrants had they lost the war," Martinell says. As written in Jack London's biography, adventure brings richness to life, and risk will always be a part of the human experience—by choice or by chance (Martinell, 2018).

Do you want choice or chance? As safety professionals and administrators, you need to think ahead and head these herd panics off at the pass.

NOTE

1. This is not a hypothetical, either; it happened to a group of students in North Ridgeville City School District outside of Cleveland, Ohio (Garcia-Navarro, 2017).

Chapter Three

Situational Awareness via Sensemaking, Your Sword and Shield

Two key concepts will come to your rescue when the torus cracks: situational awareness and sensemaking. Sensemaking is the key to functioning in chaos; situational awareness is the foundation of sensemaking. Together they create a "gut feeling" that can be at least as useful as logical deductions during a disaster.

SENSEMAKING

Sensemaking is the process of mental mapmaking we use to try to explain to ourselves what we have done and what other people are up to—especially when their behavior doesn't make sense. We try to find links between unexpected occurrences and mismatched cues.

Most scholars who talk about sensemaking are rooted in Weick's (1995) debunking of our common perception about rationalization. Intuitively, we tend to think of our decision-making process thus: we decide consciously what the best thing to do is first, and then we act.

But Weick claims the process is probably the exact opposite. First we act, based on rational and irrational impulses plus outside cues; later we look back and reverse engineer some logical-sounding reasons. We then convince ourselves that this was in fact our plan from the start (Weick, 1995).

Evolution saddled us with this ability to act before we think—and then feel fine about it—for a reason: if we sat around coming up with a rational explanation for our behavior before acting, in many crisis situations we would act too late to save ourselves.

However, if we want to understand what's going on around us well enough to act optimally, we need to be able to look past our own rationalizations as well as those around us. We need to make a habit of it without being overcome by the habit. In other words, we need a balance between being self-aware enough to understand how our own baloney might be affecting our decision-making and being too self-analytical to trust our gut feelings.

SITUATIONAL AWARENESS

Sensemaking requires data to make sense of, and so it is entirely dependent on a person's keen perception of their surroundings. This state of outward perception is known as *situational awareness*.

When office workers "prairie dog" in their cubicles—this is when there's a noise, such as an argument breaking out, or they smell doughnuts, and all the little heads pop up above the dividers like prairie dogs—they aren't just being nosy. They are displaying situational awareness.

Situational awareness is the sensory input and other knowledge that leads you to have a "gut feeling," while sensemaking consists of acknowledging that gut feeling and then rapidly evaluating a menu of reactions to the unsettling stimuli. We rationalize sensemaking into words or gestures in order to explain it to ourselves but also to share it with others ("Run northeast, Godzilla is coming from the southwest!") (Weick, Sutcliffe, & Obstfeld, 2005).

Situational awareness in the moment should be one of the top components of emergency training: knowing where you are, the actions of others, and environmental cues, such as a crack of thunder. We assume we practice vigilant awareness of our surroundings, but the fact is that our brains are designed to tune out most stimuli. Think about taking a walk. How much attention do you pay to trees, birds, a humming power pole transformer, cars passing by, or cracks in the pavement?

In most cases, hyperattention to detail isn't necessary and would exhaust us. We are efficient at monitoring a baseline, which is typically our torus. To a varying degree, each of us detects disturbances to the baseline—such as that crack of thunder that signals us to high-tail it to shelter before the onset of a storm.

When you run a fire drill, you are teaching students where the exits are—but you should also teach situational awareness. When you critique your group's performance after a drill or disaster, keep the idea of sensemaking in mind: ask yourself whether you are really describing what happened and what people were thinking or whether you are reverse engineering a flattering narrative. It's what your brain likes to do, so keep it on a short leash.

It also likes a *stable* narrative.

Remember the workers who tragically stayed at their desks minutes after Tower One was struck by a plane. Despite being alerted to danger, we press the override button in our minds because, *Meh, quit bothering me, must finish spreadsheet.*

It sounds crazy, except remember as well that people are energy-saving machines. We are awareness machines as well; it is a paradox that 9/11 brought into sharp focus.

It was confusing and terrifying, with an endless onslaught of unwanted stimuli to digest—and people react to situations in unusual ways. There is no "typical response," even among soldiers who train for hours on end, drilling survival skills and carrying out objectives in a chaotic environment.

The hard-wired system people run on is troublesome enough. But a new wrinkle has degraded situational awareness for students: smartphones. They create what is known as "focus lock."

EXERCISES: FIGHTING FOCUS LOCK

Focus lock is what happens when someone is so engrossed in texting that he or she walks into oncoming traffic. That wasn't a thing in 2001.

Fortunately, there are exercises you can do with students to counteract this effect.

The following will stick in their memories, even if it is—in fact, *because* it is—a "gotcha." People tend to remember things when they've been shown that they are incorrect (Roediger & Finn, 2010). And even before the advent of the smartphone, focus lock, and the personal social media bubble, this exercise was great at getting students to notice—at the price of some mild embarrassment for those who were book smart—that we are habitually dull when it comes to noticing what's around us.

So walk your students around the school building and school grounds for ten minutes. Tell them they can get an easy A for the day: their only job is to pay attention to their surroundings.

Unbeknownst to them, you have hidden a couple of strange items around campus: a stuffed unicorn hanging from the flagpole, a discrete wireless speaker playing "Jingle Bells" beneath a piece of playground equipment, or a silly figure sketched in sidewalk chalk—use your imagination.

After the walk, ask them, via a show of hands, whether they've perceived anything odd. A surprising number of classes will contain zero students who raise their hands. If there are one or two students who noticed your gag items, ask them to be quiet. With an infuriating little smile, walk the students back to the principal's car they just strolled past with a cardboard cutout of Justin Bieber sitting in the driver's seat.

The students will be embarrassed, but you've trained a light on their habitual tunnel vision. Repeat this exercise next week and they will be looking under every bush trying to be the "person who noticed."

Eventually, you'll be able to stretch their abilities and they will begin to notice the unusual and also the mundane around them.

This is a variation on "Kim's Game," an environmental awareness exercise that has been played for nearly a century by Boy Scouts, Girl Scouts, and even military snipers—the guys who spend the day searching through a scope for the tip of a pen wiggling in an acre of turf.

In his book *Scouting Games*, Sir Robert Baden-Powell, the founder of Scouting, describes Kim's Game as follows:

> The Scoutmaster should collect on a tray a number of articles—knives, spoons, pencil, pen, stones, book and so on—not more than about fifteen for the first few games, and cover the whole over with a cloth. He then makes the others sit round, where they can see the tray, and uncovers it for one minute. Then each of them must make a list on a piece of paper of all the articles he can remember. . . . The one who remembers most wins the game. (Baden-Powell, 2018)

If Sir Robert Baden-Powell were still around, it would be unsurprising to find him developing geocaching games, another safety teaching possibility. Unfortunately, this may present legal problems in some districts, but you can invent variations that remain within the boundaries of your classroom, school, and/or legal constraints.

Chapter Four

Legacy Knowledge

So far we have focused on an individual's torus. But schools have bagels too. It is useful and quite worthwhile to preserve the size and strength of an entire institution's torus from one generation to another.

LEGACY KNOWLEDGE

Legacy knowledge is slightly different from institutional memory, which you will recall from the introductory lesson.

Institutional memory is your school's hive mind—in a good way. It's everything an institution knows about itself via its staff: the ins and outs, big and small, that old staff can hand down to new.

Take a student who is complaining that he isn't learning the same things about particle physics that his older brother learned five years ago. His teacher is at a loss: she has only been there since last year. A teacher who has been at the school for ten years knows where to find the cache of copies of the science text they used before the new edition came out, and she shows the new teacher where to find it for reference.

Many schools neglect this transmission, firing poorly performing teachers rather than training them properly in the first place.

They could also pay a salary that would attract better staff. But instead they've spent that money on bad safety ideas: bulletproof window films, devices that detect gunshots, and app-based threat reporting systems that have never been through research trials.

This is not great budgeting. But as important as institutional knowledge is, legacy knowledge goes deeper: it is the professional knowledge that is passed down through families.

Not so long ago, the norm was that crafts and professions were hereditary, not decided via a bubble sheet test administered by your high school guidance counselor.

This is another lesson of the 9/11 rescue: though it sadly pokes yet another hole in the "ragtag crew" mythos, many of the captains and crew involved were descendants of captains and crew, who were descended from sailors, who were the descendants of the first guy in every civilization who wondered whether you could stand on something that was floating.

It wasn't a job they did for a paycheck; their family crest was a boat.

Our hypothetical here can be that nobody wants people crushed back into professional castes . . . but they *were* good for the hive. Seamen, shoemakers, and educators learned a breadth and depth of information (and took hard, brutal, but helpful criticism) about the profession that only someone who has known you since you were two cells has the time, opportunity, and emotional connection to teach.

How to replace legacy knowledge in schools? That is the $64,000 question (or $640,000 after inflation). Likely, the answer lies in strengthening institutional knowledge. Which means replacing bulletproof films with teacher training.

Thanks to free platforms like YouTube, for instance, and the fact that everybody has a movie studio in their telephone, the tech exists to allow outgoing staff to leave instructional videos for incoming staff. This means institutional knowledge gets passed down even if their terms of service do not overlap.

Further, these platforms mean that the school need not invest in the design labor that would have been necessary to create a teacher education website back in the day.

In fact, the cost of creating an entire library of instructional YouTube videos left on a completely private channel for your staff would be (well, assuming there's already a camera on each staffer's laptop, as is currently standard, and they're on salary) $0. That beats a bulletproof film by infinity.

In more ways than one: Do you want to pay inflated, "For the children!" prices to get slightly less breakable windows or a staff that has access to the sum total of past institutional knowledge? And don't overlook an opportunity to improve the induction process for staff and students that join your school community after the first day of class. Through recorded training and mentors, you can inform them about "the way safety things are done around here."

Teaching the torus is the most important item in school safety. Bar none.

The good thing about this fact is that a torus comes free with the human operating system. The bad thing is, you can't buy an upgrade for your staff and students—not at any price. You have to figure out a way to get them to earn an upgrade.

Once upon a time, legacy knowledge did much of the work for you.

The intimate details of a staff member's job might have been part of her torus since birth (and we wouldn't call her "a staff member," we would call her "Jenny's daughter Josie"). In the days we live in, we have to get creative.

There's more than one way to bake a bagel.

Part II

The Foolishness of Benchmarking

Chapter Five

Disasters Are the Real Snowflakes

So now you understand why people do weird things in a crisis: we cling to the familiar, even at the expense of our lives.

Think of the hundreds of Twin Towers employees on 9/11 who stayed at their desks for minutes after an airplane slammed into the building (Ripley, 2008). Many were saving their documents; some even shut down their computers.

How many people died that day because they were too slow to realize their world had changed? Granted, they couldn't see the television images; they didn't know what hit them. But being fair minded doesn't bring them back.

IF YOU KNEW NOW WHAT YOU KNOW NOW

Although today's kids might have smaller bagels than the 9/11 generation, safety-minded educators do have one advantage over the past: we know that there *is* a bagel. We know more about how minds work and how to hack them.

So why aren't we using that information?!

The same psychological force that paralyzes people in a crisis is freezing the safety profession. To keep the ball rolling, we must design training and systems to compensate for human glitchiness. We need to teach people to confront their tendency to freeze. But instead we are indulging in it ourselves. We freeze like deer in headlights—or like wifi techs who are scared of computers.

Instead of reading the literature that tells them this information, safety professionals keep drawing a paycheck by designing ever more elaborate drills based on the latest crisis.

Trouble is, the next crisis is not going to look like the last crisis.

Nobody drilled for 9/11 . . . because nobody had ever seen anything like it. And the likelihood of the next major crisis actually resembling 9/11 is low.

As those who create threats to our normalcy continue to think further and further outside the box, we as safety pros must think outside the bagel.

For example, the design of active shooter drills almost always assumes there will be one shooter because that's been the majority of shootings.

Fine, but you've trained people to be linear and do what they've been told, particularly when they're unfamiliar with being outside of their bagels, so what happens when five shooters show up? Or if they show up with a homemade nuke? What if they have a drone providing cover fire?

Your resources can surprise you too. What if volunteer rescuers show up offering drones of their own? Will you be flexible enough to incorporate them or will you turn them down because they aren't part of the plan?

You can't teach your staff and students every currently conceivable situation, much less the inconceivable situation that's surely down the line.

This doesn't stop some professionals from trying. They belong to the "mile wide and an inch deep" school of thought; they are the reason one school had a hefty scenario binder with highlights that included disasters like "Plane Falls Out of Sky."

If you can teach them to adapt and process chaos, they'll have the best chance to survive in this state of chaos. If you can't, well . . .

Many safety professionals want to believe that the next crisis will, in fact, resemble a past crisis and that we can create a very specific and detailed plan to be ready for it.

Alas, no dice. You can't ignore past crises, but the lessons we draw from them must be general principles not specific solutions. You can't benchmark the future to past crises, and you can't prescribe detailed instructions for every possibility.

Instead take the middle path of curiosity and measured comparisons. Without benchmarking *or* ignoring the past, this lets you use others' experience without getting lost in it.

So we return to Manhattan.

LOWER MANHATTAN: GEOGRAPHY AND DEMOGRAPHY

Why and how did followers decide to obey other people in order to safely evacuate Manhattan Island?

The neighborhoods immediately around the site of the 9/11 attacks are known as "Lower Manhattan": fourteen census tracts south of Canal Street, encompassing the Financial District, Battery Park City, Tribeca, the Civic Center, and a chunk of Chinatown. Manhattan is also an island that is bridged to the mainland. As such, comparisons of the Manhattan Island rescue to nonisland rescues have been fervently attempted and fail to capture the unique challenges inherent only to a population dense island.

In 2000, Lower Manhattan was overwhelmingly white non-Hispanic (63 percent) and Asian non-Hispanic (27 percent). The profile of Lower Manhattan residents showed a group with high levels of education, occupational skills, and income. Nearly 69 percent of those working in Lower Manhattan lived in the five boroughs of New York City, while 31 percent commuted from suburban counties. The largest industry grouping in Lower Manhattan was FIRE (finance, insurance, and real estate), which employed 151,200 workers or 39 percent of the workforce. Management positions numbered 182,700 and accounted for 47 percent of all workers in Lower Manhattan (Salvo et al., 2007).

Next let's talk more in-depth about the psychology of the people involved in these disasters: even if 9/11 reoccurred tomorrow, the rescue could not be the same because the people we would be rescuing would not be the same. This means we have to talk about a concept from another discipline. We've been stealing bagels out of chaos theory; time to steal from Freud. We're going to talk about the transference dynamic.

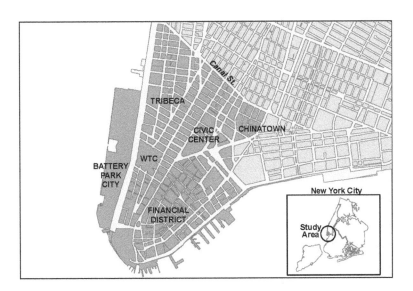

Figure 5.1. Lower Manhattan study area. Used with permission of the New York City Department of City Planning. All rights reserved. *Source: Salvo et al., 2007.*

Chapter Six

Another New Latin Word

Psychological Transference

Transference combines two old Latin roots: "trans," which means "across," and the verb "fer," which means "to carry." Carry across. The transference dynamic is another way of saying that an emotion you have learned to attach to one thing or person can be carried over to a similar thing or person later in life.

Freud postulated the transference dynamic in the early twentieth century to describe a curious if potentially flattering phenomenon: his patients kept falling in love with him, even the men. He was puzzled, as he knew he wasn't an Adonis or even very nice. He decided instead that he was becoming a substitute dad. Unlike their real fathers, in many cases, he was listening to the clients and trying to help. He was filling the role that many people wish their father would fill.

So they saw in him the idealized image of a perfect father. He was not only the object of transference, he was better than the original. They projected all manner of positive character traits onto him, particularly traits they had encountered before or strongly wished to encounter. Freud realized this happened in many love relationships: whether their parents were awful and they wanted a nice mom for once, or whether they were perfect and irreplaceable, people would seek to find the perfect parent in everyone they latched onto.

The transference dynamic does not stop at love and therapy; later researchers and therapists have applied it to a broad range of transferences. Business management scholars have noticed that transference occurs with business leaders: if a manager finds a way to remind employees of somebody fabulous, it will become easy for her to inspire unforced obedience.

On the darker side, this can also inspire an enthused embrace of unpaid overtime or other abuses, both at work and in relationships; manipulative people are experts at exploiting transference.

On the good side, transference helps us follow well-meaning but imperfect leaders: followers who are experiencing transference are likely to think, "This is very difficult and John has made a mistake, but he's one of the smartest people I know. Surely he will get us through."

Transference doesn't stop at human relationships; it applies to situations and institutions. In fact, institutional transference is even more important than leader transference. One situation reminds us of another. And in a crisis, if a person is used to feeling he or she can depend on institutions in general, he or she is likely to have more trust in whatever impromptu system springs up to deal with an unfolding crisis.

This is another demographic difference between the 9/11 harbor rescuees and our current students: on 9/11, the average person involved in the crisis was born around 1960 (Salvo et al., 2007).

They had seen the U.S. government send people to the moon when they were nine years old—a feat unequaled in current students' time. Our current space program mostly centers on servicing cell phone satellites so kids can send each other threatening tweets.

The 9/11 rescuees were used to the government promising to keep them safe from the Russians, progressively introducing programs such as the Star Wars initiative. The Vietnam War was a blemish, but then again America's heroic victory in World War II still dominated the collective consciousness. And the spectre of 9/11 (and the unwinnable wars it triggered) wasn't haunting us yet.

When they saw the impromptu fleet pulling into the harbor as Manhattan collapsed, their hearts rose: their fellow Americans had cobbled together a system, and they had faith that it would work.

Would our current students trust that fleet? Would they trust each other not to stampede for the boats? Or would they stand in Battery Park transfixed?

Many researchers think of transference as a purely subconscious phenomenon, a mere gut feeling we can't control that bubbles up from the depths of our minds unbidden under stress.

However, Rory Miller's work with prison guards is worth a read. Miller sees transference as something that you can train your mind to recognize as it is occurring—move it from the subconscious to the conscious. This means you have some control over the speed at which you accept the transference impulse.

Another way of talking about the transference dynamic sounds a bit like evolutionary psychology . . . which it sort of is, but we're not going to use it to talk about pickup artistry and electoral politics, which is unfortunately becoming the common use of "evolutionary psychology."

Admiral Loy, as he called together the fleet on 9/11, was an example of what psychology calls an "alpha," a leader who organically emerges in a group as a pecking order develops. Loy was already formally an admiral, but he also became a heartily accepted authority. Behind him an equally organic subhierarchy of harbor captains also developed as the rescue unfolded.

But times change. If you were forty in 2001, there was no shame in following a natural or ordained leader, as long as he or she was credible enough to be the target of transference. People were comfortable with either following a leader or striking out on their own.

Today, students have had "teamwork" and "consensus building" shoved down their throats so relentlessly (by a hierarchy of educators who, ironically, order them to not be hierarchical) that they are no longer capable of either making decisions for themselves *or* of following an alpha.

When you assert yourself as an individual, you are labeled a bully, and on any given subject, the group as a whole or a charismatic scold has more authority than . . . an authority.

In other words, youth aren't going to respond to an alpha adult *or* an alpha peer, however organic. The smartphone is their alpha; the tribe—or even more often the Internet—is the object of the transference dynamic, with everyone searching frantically for an online consensus.

If they're millennial age or younger, people seem to have almost entirely replaced meat tribes with phone tribes. Phone addiction is pandemic among youth (and fogeys aren't far behind). This is as dangerous when you need fast thinking as it is when you need special knowledge, not just an online consensus. People who know a lot about the situation become alphas for a reason.

For example, in the 1980s, kids from all over the city would habitually show up at a playlot at 8:00 in the morning. The older kids divided the teams and made accommodations as circumstances warranted.

Then, in the 1990s, adults barged in and organized the sandlot activities, adding participation trophies and other feel-good tedium—we didn't even have regular trophies, just bragging rights!—and kids got fed up with it.

Today, the sandlots are empty. Kids sit in front of video games, getting fat and crazy, and following game rules that an unknown adult a thousand miles away laid out for them.

Ironically, by forcing them all to be equal, we've taken away their rights to recognize their own natural leaders. It's a tragic loss of something precious.

It's also a safety hazard: consensus is pretty, but when you are trapped in a cave, you follow the guy or girl who can read the map.

The trick is distinguishing the natural leader from the loud person who is *pretending* to know the way out. People's instincts in this area can be surprisingly accurate under stress, but their chances of following the right leader are better if they understand the dynamics involved. That is why our students desperately need to learn about the torus.

Normally, kids develop a kind of situational awareness, and an awareness of the obvious when it comes to social relationships, fairly early in their growth. Ask any kindergarten class who is the fastest runner and all hands shoot up with a harmonious "I am!"

Ask that same question to those kids three years later and, without hesitation, they point to Marcus. That's the reality; Marcus blazes around the gymnasium. If you're on his team in kickball, you're in luck because Marcus can stretch a single into a double. But it's also counter to teaching all kids that they are all equal and all capable of all things.

A few years later, the kids have learned to hesitate when asked this question. Point to Marcus at your own risk because that's elitist.

In some strange sense, education has turned splinter strengths into micro-aggressions. You know what they say in Japan: "The nail that sticks out shall be hammered down."

Educators think this is good for kids socially. And maybe in some situations it is. But what we are really telling kids is that *transference is bad*. Knowing the obvious is bad. Knowing who the natural leaders are is bad. Which won't fly in a crisis situation.

If we have high school–aged kids who are still all sticking their hands up like kindergarteners and yelling, "We're all the fastest!" then the kids will just stand there in a clump, afraid to make decisions or appoint a leader, while they are picked off one by one.

Educators need to rethink this blind commitment to equality. Students must know *before* disaster strikes that they will not be punished for sensing who is ready to step up to the plate. This is a delicate subject and must be approached with tact and care. But it must be approached. The question is how.

You could make an appeal to authority: How about Dr. Paul Rapp? He was kind enough to aid with the first draft of this book. Rapp is a professor of military and emergency medicine at the Uniformed Services University and director of the Traumatic Injury Research Program.

He also holds a secondary appointment as a professor of medical and clinical psychology. He starred in *The Strange New Science of Chaos*, which aired on NOVA in 1989, arguing that chaotic behavior—going with the flow, dude—can have massive functional advantages.

These ideas have aged well and are still useful in promoting fast, solid decision-making in schools during times of chaos.

Rapp is one of a handful of psychoanalytically trained mathematicians in the world, which affords him deep insight into transference. Here's a member check for you: contra the thesis of this chapter, Rapp doesn't think the 9/11 boat rescue was about transference—he warns against overgeneralizing. His ideas about transference make a complementary counterpart to this book.

"I would not consider what happened to these people, and their rational behavior in an irrational environment, as transference as it is precisely defined," he said, because transference is an *unconscious* process; instead the 9/11 rescuees consciously decided to defer to Admiral Loy's competence. "I speculate these people were making a conscious decision to trust," mostly because their "number of options had collapsed."

From previous chapters, you likely got the impression that the rescue fleet was a romantically ragtag crew à la *Star Wars*. But though Han Solo may not have begun as an official militia member, he still was an accomplished flyer.

Which means his underlings didn't need much expertise. "I've seen this in medical emergency situations," Rapp says. "If you have a really experienced leader on an ambulance crew, everybody just sort of falls into line and things work out well" (Rapp, personal interview, 2017).

These are two ways of getting to the same basic point: listen to your gut because gut instincts develop over time. The question is whether the process can be hurried. "Rather than transference," says Rapp, "are we observing a psychological capacity developed unconsciously over a long period of maturation that leads to the ability to consciously decide to accept competent leadership?"

Whether it began as a transference dynamic or a conscious choice, this should all end with your eyes wide open to the world: Be conscious about being conscious about your gut instinct. It's a bit meta, but with a modicum of training it can become . . . well, fairly instinctual.

However, although basically arguing the same point, it is of interest to note that Dr. Rapp's divergence with the position espoused in this book takes us into the realm of epistemology, or the inquiry into what distinguishes justified belief from opinion. Much of the safety industry would be improved if people took off the rose-colored glasses and tried some different tints of epistemology—be it empiricism (as seen in this book) or constructivism, which is scientific knowledge obtained by humans measuring and interacting with the real world.

One pitfall with a strong belief in empiricism is that it tends to use history and what is proven to be real—which is good, but this doesn't help us leap way out to new thinking and new creations, like constructivist thinking, or even way, way out there stuff like postmodern thinking.

That's a limitation to being an empiricist—you tend to move slowly and refine what is known—so to get from the ice box to the refrigerator takes a generation, whereas a constructivist might get there in a couple of years. If you step into constructivism, however, you trade off a known trend line and history of something that is proven to venture out into something that hasn't proven itself. Not that this is bad; Rapp is a good example of a thinker who is a bit more constructivist compared to others who are more inclined toward empiricism. We need all the honest lines of inquiry we can get in this field; unfortunately, too many people aren't interested in honest inquiry, whatever their methods. Far too many people involved with safety are afraid to stop repeating the party line. Most are acting like a broken Roomba, cleaning and recleaning the single corner of the house where the entire profession has gotten stuck. It is now way past time to knock it off!

Chapter Seven

So What's Wrong with Benchmarking?

Critical Decision-Making in a Nonlinear World

So by now you can see the safety problems generated by not just conformity within the profession but also the very nice idea of universal equality. If you ignore individuals' special talents, you're taking the helpful impulse for transference and throwing it out the window; if you can't break away from your colleagues, you'll never have the guts to deal with the fallout from that idea.

Most safety professionals and textbooks *love* benchmarking, or at least they have historically. Hopefully, this book can help accelerate the beginnings of change in this department as well.

To review, benchmarking is the practice of assuming that one crisis is going to be much like another, despite the passage of time, different places, and shifting circumstances. This usually means using a past crisis as a "benchmark" to which we slavishly nail our predictions and practices for the same category of disaster (shooter, flood, Godzilla) in the future. By now, you can probably recite the short answer for why this is wrong: technology changes, populations and their transference histories and toruses (tori?) change, and the arms race among terrorists, climate change, and safety professionals is ongoing.

But you want to be sure this is not all a mere thought and logic experiment, correct? So let's look deeper into the pros and cons of comparing one crisis to another. There are lessons to learn from looking at past disasters, but they aren't in the similarities, they're in the differences. One of the main lessons of Lower Manhattan is that lessons cannot be taken too particularly. The actors in that rescue were substantially different from those involved in the Oklahoma City bombing or from any school shooting.

49

Of course, even if people aren't merely a constant variable, an evacuation is still an evacuation, right? Just because Gen Z has a small torus doesn't mean they can't walk down a flight of stairs the same way as anyone else. Why can't these situations be treated the same? Transference plays a huge part in it, as even differences between past generations will show. But so does technology and so do other developments and variables.

Schools forget to look inside their own bagel for their baseline and to improve the practices that work, or would work, for their unique context and situation and instead seek to copy practices from what are often urban schools—and wealthy schools. They see the safety "bling" and feel they need it.

At best a school can mimic another school. But that's pretty tricky for a rural school district with five hundred students whose average local taxpayer has a $70,000 home if they're trying to benchmark to a metropolitan school district that serves twenty-five thousand students with a tax base full of million-dollar apartments.

RESCUE RECIPIENTS: THE DIFFERENCE BETWEEN THEN AND NOW

Different rescuees also make for a completely different situation. Those rescued from Lower Manhattan accounted for 47 percent of all workers in the area (Salvo et al., 2007). Their average age was forty; they were educated and familiar with their environment. Your students may have trouble with developing a useful transference dynamic in an emergency, but improvement is not impossible. In fact, earlier generations, such as those who lived through World War II, might have thought the same thing about the 9/11 generation, at least in terms of their being afraid of bogeymen.

These rescuees had not been raised to be fearless warriors; far from it. On June 1, 1980, Cable News Network (CNN) debuted as the world's first twenty-four-hour television news network. It was now possible for Americans to view real-time disasters, emergencies, and saber-rattling from communist countries. A year later, the United States orbited the space shuttle Columbia and demonstrated dominance in the space race.

The typical forty year old rescued on 9/11 would have been graduating college as the terrifying nuclear war film *The Day After* was viewed by more than one hundred million people on ABC in 1983—a movie that undoubtedly made their parents flash back to the days the world teetered on apocalypse during the Cuban Missile Crisis.

Also in 1983, President Reagan proposed the Strategic Defense Initiative (SDI) in an address to the nation. SDI was a futuristic missile defense system intended to protect the United States from attack by ballistic strategic nuclear weapons. SDI was nicknamed "Star Wars." This grandiose plan also tilted standing sentiment from mutually assured destruction (MAD) to presumed first strike, hence portraying the Soviets as contemplating first strike. The Soviets escalated their military posture, including developing their first and only space shuttle, Buran. This was in the news and stitched into song lyrics. In the early 1980s, international conflict was on everyone's mind.

Pop culture also reflected the generation's concerns about war. In 1984, singer Nena released the hit song "99 Red Balloons," an antiwar protest song against NATO nuclear missile deployments. Sting released "Russians" in 1985, a song with a haunting melody including the phrase "I hope the Russians love their children." That same year American boxer Rocky Balboa (Sylvester Stallone), protagonist of Western values, defeated the fierce Russian opponent Ivan Drago (Dolph Lundgren) in the blockbuster film *Rocky IV*, a movie with thick references to Cold War tensions, hinting that the Soviets would exploit all means to topple the United States. It's a wonder that the military didn't shatter recruitment quotas as young patriots exiting theaters were ready to punch out the first Russki that crossed their path!

However, all of these were external bogeymen. This generation did *not* grow up with the fear that the kid in the desk next to them might show up with a gun and a backpack full of grenades next Wednesday, nor were they told that going to the park alone would surely end in a kidnapping and a dungeon, or at the very least a citation for their parents for neglect. They had more trust for the people and institutions around them and thus were more likely to see benevolence, possibility, and a likely positive outcome in the rescue as it developed.

Students now are very different, as you have seen. However, it's not just demographics that change from one disaster to another. We have mentioned that ever-evolving arms race between shooters/terrorists and safety professionals; conditions on any given day are going to be different, whether it's the weather or traffic patterns. In fact, any of a nearly infinite number of unpredictable factors can turn what seems like a familiar type of crisis into a whole new ball game. Instead of trying to guess where the ball is going to be hit ahead of time, we need to set up our defense to play any ball.

Chapter Eight

Why Comparing Disasters Feels Too Good to Be True

We have not served the kids of this generation well—when it comes to surviving disasters or even when it comes to navigating life—and that we need to do better. If we teach them to expand their bagels, this will also serve them well in the working world, relationships, and in their relationships with themselves.

Now let's look at the other specific circumstances that unfold unpredictably. Here the example of 9/11 itself will serve to illustrate why benchmarking one disaster to another is of such very limited use.

The response to the attacks on the World Trade Center complex was not per a planned and measured drill or experiment and therefore lacked design, baseline, objective and subjective measurement tools, and controls over the introduction of noise to the system. In other words, nobody could stand around saying, "Well, the last twenty times someone flew an airplane into a skyscraper, X seemed to work out pretty well. . . ." (For these reasons, finite details could be debated to infinity.)

The 9/11 boat rescue is frequently compared to the World War II evacuation of the British Expeditionary Force and other Allied troops from the French seaport of Dunkirk. Naval vessels and hundreds of civilian boats were used in that evacuation, which began on May 26, 1940. When it ended on June 4, 1940, about 198,000 British and 140,000 French and Belgian troops had been saved (Dunkirk Evacuation, 2018). While astonishing, the Dunkirk evacuation was situated in a vastly different context six decades before the World Trade Center attacks. Events are laminated to contexts, situations, geography, demography, and time, even if the emotions evoked by the narrative of one situation resemble the archetypal responses of another.

Indeed, the drama and narrative satisfaction of Dunkirk and Lower Manhattan are very much alike—*We're going to be like Dunkirk too!*

As part of the transference dynamic, such self-edification is not without its uses, and this narrative may indeed be helpful in instilling confidence in leadership to students who very much need it.

However, for your own benefit—for the purposes of figuring out how to strategize around safety behind the scenes as opposed to storytelling or self-edifying—it is not as useful to juxtapose Dunkirk and New York City, nor to compare the 9/11 attacks to other attacks.

The conventional wisdom about school safety is counterfactual and misleading in ways that are very similar to the ways in which conventional wisdom about 9/11 is counterfactual and misleading. The accepted story is that the rescuers who pulled up to Manhattan in boats were magic, and the major media conducted things majestically, giving all the right cues from on high.

No one tells you how lucky they were—when it came to the weather, the time of day, and even the range of years when most of the rescuees were born. If it had been snowing or if Manhattan was full of millennials, the event would have unfolded completely differently, and anyone who attempted a rescue would probably have been seen in a less flattering light.

Studies per this constant comparison mold have nonetheless been conducted ad nauseam, and findings tend to converge upon the same set of problems to be solved: command, communications, planning, resource management, and public relations. Unfortunately, all events are specific to a moment in time. The findings of all these studies are linear in nature—they offer the comforting illusion that they lend themselves to being remedied by fiddling with a particular knob in the system ahead of time.

But the planning that works for one shooter, to go back to our simplest example, has to be tossed out when there are three shooters, particularly if they enter the area at different points and times. Your plan is in motion for the shooter who came in the front door of the school, just like last time . . . and suddenly someone is on the roof, rappelling down to a third-floor window (not to give them any ideas).

Chapter Nine

One Variable, One Very Big Difference

The Internet

Here is another specific example of how each event is marked by geography and demography and particularly time. Oklahoma City is a case that is constantly benchmarked to 9/11, compared and contrasted as case studies in emergency response plans. The Alfred P. Murrah Building in Oklahoma City was mauled by a domestic truck bombing on April 19, 1995, resulting in 168 total deaths.

You can interview responders, qualitatively code recorded communications, and make every effort to assemble the shattered pieces of evidence into a meaningful mosaic. However, if you change one variable about the historical context of a disaster, this makes a surprisingly large difference in the way a given type of situation unfolds. Per Internet World Stats (2018), in 1995, sixteen million people, or 0.4 percent of the world's population, used the Internet via bulky desktop units with boxy monitors. In 2018, an estimated 55 percent of the world's population used the Internet—and mobile devices surpass desktops!

"So what?" you might think. But this means that the availability of and ability to communicate information were much greater for rescuers and recipients in the 2001 WTC attacks relative to their counterparts in the 1995 bombing. The world learned about the Murrah Building bombing from television. Americans learned of the WTC attacks from Yahoo. This improvement in communication wasn't due to strategic changes in safety planning after the 1995 bombing, but rather it was secondary to overall advances in telecommunication systems.

Cell phones also shot up in usage, capability, and reliability, and since 2001 they have improved again. Recent hurricanes have compromised, but have not disabled, cellular towers. When voice communications failed, the towers continued to transmit personal text messages.

The great curiosity of the 9/11 boat rescue is that it defies the traditional problems forensically identified in rescue efforts, such as communication, command, and public relations. None of these expected impediments hampered or even really affected the boat rescue, even as the Incident Command System (ICS) melted down on land.

So although they continually try to benchmark new events to 9/11, most safety professionals are puzzled as to why the rescue wasn't a massive failure. Everything they think about disasters fails to apply to this landmark rescue . . . and yet they keep trying to use 9/11 as a model for new situations. Are you starting to see the problem here?

To figure out why Admiral Loy's nonplan did not crash and burn, studies of the boat rescue have centered on chaos, problem solving, and improvisation. While contributing to the knowledge base of the rescue event, researchers of the 9/11 boat rescue ignore the transference dynamic, as well as pareidolia—another key (and related) mechanism that led to the fast-moving rescue of half a million people; this will be discussed in chapter 19.

Chapter Ten

A Final Word on Schools and Benchmarking

One really tragic flaw in the preoccupation with benchmarking is that it ignores the differences between schools. If you must benchmark things, it seems logical that you should at least be able to benchmark one school to another.

Alas, this, too, is fatally flawed logic. As much as we have bemoaned the inequality of educational opportunities across class backgrounds in our country, the fact remains: schools are unequal. There are budgetary, as well as many other, factors that set every school apart from every other. Even during the same year, and even if you could replicate the same crisis—number of shooters, strategy, etc.—no two schools are going to have the same needs.

A rural school district with five hundred students is vastly different from a metropolitan school district that serves twenty-five thousand students. Nobody benchmarks to the small rural schools—everyone benchmarks to the big schools.

Benchmarking in schools is simply copying what someone else is doing—something that looks like it is better because a good school does it and it has been hailed as a standard of progress in safety. But adapting it directly doesn't account for the fact that the school you are benchmarking to pays teachers more and thus has higher retention and more institutional memory; the root issue is not those sparkly new security cameras, it's the fact that you can't offer the same teacher pay.

Look at your own baseline and how to improve it with what you have. The answer is almost always teach the torus, and . . . drill fidelity. Drill fidelity is what we are about to tackle in the next chapter, so keep reading.

Part III

Drill Fidelity

The fire alarms at a school for blind children went off five minutes into lunch on a Friday. Staff and students were efficiently exiting the building—even though it meant abandoning their lunch trays. Nobody conducts a drill during lunchtime or, for that matter, as students arrive or depart or recess or during assemblies or on Grandparents' Day. So no one knew quite what to think.

Moments later, sirens and air horns penetrated the building as aerial, pumper, and rescue trucks were rumbling down our street. The cat was out of the bag. This was authentic. A fire at the School for the Blind.

The fire department made sure the building had been cleared. They then sought out the ranking administrator and head of maintenance to debrief them on their assessment of the situation and also to obtain information about the building. That didn't take long. The firefighters went about their business, and staff and students waited at the established perimeter. There was no need to activate some complex multistep safety response plan or go deep into layers of the school incident command structure.

It was a remarkably beautiful warm day. A second alarm brought additional firefighters and apparatus to the school. Firefighters needed to ventilate smoke from the building and diligently assess the roof and vents for smoldering debris. An hour later, the incident was over. Firefighters departed, the maintenance crew worked to remove a roasted industrial dryer, and kids were on their way home. Buses that normally picked kids up at the school had staged a block away—not a big deal.

Now, a few things to note. Nobody would ever recommend conducting a spontaneous safety drill five minutes into lunch on a Friday at the School for the Blind—or, for that matter, any other school. When do fire drills happen? During good weather. Run a fire drill in the rain and you'll draw the ire of parents, staff, and students.

The following week, the principal and a teacher met with four separate groups composed of a total of six to eight students and staff. Each group met for forty minutes in the conference room. They asked them about the fire— what they did, what they thought, what went well, what didn't go well. A staffer took four pages of notes for each session and then coded them. This is called qualitative interviewing—information gathering and then finding themes. It blows surveys out of the water. Staff and students stated that the alarm was not frightening, although it was peculiar to have it go off when it did. They also said that because they were drilled often they knew what to do.

But this wasn't as linear as it appears. Not everyone was in the lunchroom. Some were in hallways. What did they do? They found doors close to them and exited the building and then proceeded to the perimeters. One added, "We knew it was best to get out of the building and then get to the safe areas—which meant walking across grass or so on." Remember, we are talking about staff and students that are blind or have significant visual disabilities. But this process of convening small groups after safety drills was something that school was used to, and students already knew that in a fire alarm they were to find the closest exit, and if it was a lockdown drill to get behind the closest door.

So standing outside for an hour wasn't a gripe from anyone, but people in each group stated that after thirty minutes, they wished that they would have been told what was going on. Just imagine being blind and hearing—and feeling, as the concrete vibrated under your feet—as another pumper rolls up to the school.

On 9/11, NYC officials did an exceptional job at giving regular updates throughout the day and repeating information that had been shared earlier that people might have missed as they evacuated. In the forensic analysis of the 9/11 harbor rescue, communication at regular intervals was a strength of the evacuation of Lower Manhattan—and not just explicit directions but communication of navy ships being dispatched to the area to protect the eastern seaboard.

Drill fidelity at that school had created a student body that, even if they couldn't see during a disaster, knew both the basics of what to do and what to do if everything didn't go according to plan, such as not getting access to the proper adaptive equipment.

So what's the takeaway here? They drilled with fidelity. They measured the effectiveness of drills via qualitative group feedback sessions and authorized staff and students to exercise discretion to act in their best interests and for the best interests of those under their care. Simply doing solid drills can remove a great deal of potential panic from most situations. The trick is to drill solidly while still preaching flexibility.

Chapter Eleven

Fancy Drills Are Worse than Useless

Specific disasters loom large in our minds. The images of those planes flying into the Twin Towers triggered a rash of panicked, crazy ideas; for example, one entrepreneur who tried to sell backpack parachutes to high-rise workers. However, 9/11 didn't make us as crazy as the highly publicized school shootings of the past few decades have.

Schools have turned to all kinds of crazy stunts. We've already mentioned the rubber bullet drills, but some schools pump up the realism to the point of absurdity, even roping in the local performing arts folks to stage paint the kids like they've been the backstop at a shooting range.

Tornadoes impact schools each year, but nobody does a drill by having kids go into the hallway, assume the crash position, and then give the custodian the nod to switch on a barn fan and chuck handfuls of gravel into it to "simulate" the experience of having debris whipped at the kids by a tornado.

It's the same with fire drills: you don't pump artificial smoke into hallways and throw debris at the exit routes to force people to problem solve alternative exits. We only pull in the drama club for school shootings.

The Institutional Review Board of any research university would swat that proposal off the table after the first page due to the obvious jeopardy to the psychological welfare of the subjects. There's a reason you can't find published studies from researchers conducting active shooter drill research in schools: the research proposals would never get off the ground because no postsecondary institution would take on the liability of such a study.

Too many drills are built on some one-time "study" funded by a safety vendor that doesn't have sufficient numbers of participants to drive a statistical confidence level. That is poor research, and it gets worse. So-called safety gurus build their entire presentations on an introductory flurry of slides with screenshots of media headlines.

The evidence for much of what is claimed to be scientific method school safety "research" is the equivalent of a clinical trial that "tests" asthma medication on five people and then generalizes claims about the findings to all asthma sufferers.

Part of research is sample size, or "n" size, and it matters, as larger n sizes contribute to validity and reliability. Good quality research is tedious and findings might not support the hypothesis. The purpose of research isn't to prove that you are correct. The purpose of research is to learn and gather evidence. That's not welcomed news if you must claim your new school safety gadget is supported by research.

One thing that must be kept in mind about drills is that real disasters can strike anytime—including during a drill.

This is a large part of why drills should be done parsimoniously; it may actually be more difficult for people to realize that the torus has been shattered when they're pretending that the torus has been shattered, not to mention the fact that large-scale drills concentrate responders in one area. This is yet another reason why one good solid general evacuation drill is worth ten sessions of LARPing a specific shooter or hurricane scenario.

Aside from being silly and superfluous, drama drills distract and detract from the core skills you are trying to teach: How do I get out of this building? What alarms will signal a crisis somewhere in the school? How do I coordinate with my teachers and classmates? What is the basic overall pattern we will follow in all making it out of here together?

If you do the drills with more urgency and less often, overall retention can improve because your students won't be shutting off their brains to endure yet another boring drill. Do you remember fire drills from your childhood? No one does.

In their study, "Accountability and Assessment of Emergency Drills at School," Ramirez, Kubicek, Peek-Asa, and Wong (2009) report that "drills were not typically recognized as a training vehicle but rather as a compulsory exercise with little meaning. Observations indicated that students, particularly in the middle and high schools, often did not evacuate in an orderly fashion (e.g., in lines) and that staff generally did not correct this behavior."

While observers recorded the amount of time it took for staff and students to evacuate a building, these figures could only be compared to local averages and not against any known recommended threshold. They also noted that students appeared desensitized to the drills. It is possible that the apathy for safety drills perceived by Ramirez was part of a larger question of students' indifference to their school. Finally, drills were not used as opportunities to adopt changes in problematic procedures.

So do what you can to give context, keep the number of drills down, and keep the students' attention so they may actually retain the information. If the leader can slip in an exercise to develop their situational awareness, all the better.

One great idea for improving engagement came from a student in a focus group. She suggested that new students to the school should get a "drill buddy" to help show them the ropes so that everything doesn't have to be explained to the entire school whenever there is a new group of students. (Considering student turnover, this is almost every drill.) This both reduces boring repetition and gives the drill buddy some investment in the learning situation. It also helps with the institutional continuity we discussed earlier.

Another crucial but simple step you can take to increase your drill fidelity is to create teaching objectives. That's a jargony way of saying you should know exactly where you're going with the drill when you design it. Begin the design by listing things that you want to teach: where the exits are, why they should use the first exit rather than the door they usually use to come in, how to cooperate with their classmates, how not to panic and stay focused, etc.

Design your drill around your teaching objectives. Forget about realistic details meant to simulate a disaster itself, whether emotionally or aesthetically. To try would be a fool's errand: you cannot simulate a disaster.

First, if you did something that was genuinely dangerous, you would traumatize students at the very least. Second, everyone knows it's a drill. You are *not* showing students what it is like to be in a real shooter situation. You are teaching them skills for use in that situation.

But schools and safety professionals alike tend more and more to insist on spending precious time and money trying to create an impossible and useless verisimilitude. People who like graphic scary drills will argue that we need to make shooter drills as "real" as possible so people "feel it in their gut" so that later they will know how to deal with panic.

But you can never wipe a student's brain clean before he or she starts a drill so he or she will believe he or she is in a real situation. These are the same kids who play ultrarealistic first-person-shooter video games in which aliens attack them in ways that are far more graphic than anything you can reproduce in a school drill. These games would be far more terrifying than your shooter drills . . . *if only the player did not know that he or she is playing a game.*

If immersive experiences were genuinely frightening, people would be exhausted after an hour of gaming. Instead, they calmly reach for their Mountain Dew for a five-hour session and then go upstairs for dinner.

There is no way to simulate danger. Do you want students to get a sample of the gamut of emotions that range up to fear? Then let them go on that field trip to DC! Let them play sandlot baseball and stay out of their way while they deal with the emotions that come up when they win, lose, or have to negotiate what compromises to make if one kid has a bad leg.

Why school officials will make an exception to their overall policy of hugboxes and safe spaces to shoot rubber bullets at their students—why *this* is the area where they choose to make an exception—is beyond me. It is a huge contradiction to build safe spaces against microaggressions when you're inviting gun-toting police or military-like simulation trainers into your school.

Not that you can't get hurt when something goes wrong doing one of these drills. In fact, the closer you get to mimicking a disaster, the closer you get to creating one.

There's the rub: a drill that goes right won't genuinely frighten anyone, but one that goes wrong can end in a lawsuit. So stop shooting rubber bullets. And for the love of God, never pretend an active shooter is in the building without telling people it's an exercise.

Believe it or not, this is also suddenly trendy—to have a masked intruder bolt into the building with a fake gun and only top administration knows it's not real. Yes, it does get around the question of how to create fear when everyone knows it's a drill. It's also a hell of a lot of fun for the safety pros involved. But it's also a great way to have Gladys the secretary pull a Pearl pistol from her purse and kill the assistant superintendent who was role-playing in a ski mask with a toy gun.

Figure 11.1. Author in SWAT gear during school intruder training. *Credit: David Perrodin.*

Chapter Twelve

The Right Way to Conduct a Drill

Critical Decision-Making in a Nonlinear World

What does your brain really sound like when the torus explodes? Kevin Sullivan of the *Wait What If Podcast* is a military veteran and finished his officer training a couple of weeks before September 11, 2001. He spent three tours in Iraq before a combat injury took him from the battlefield and into the classroom where he became a physician's assistant. Kevin shared a time when he was under heavy shelling while on a runway.

Military scientists expect pounced-on soldiers to apply what they learned from drills and models. This phenomenon is known as selecting the available heuristic, or decision-making shortcut, and it often fails as brains are overrun with input stimuli and flailing to find some recognizable pattern, some anchor, from which to base the next move.

Per Kevin, the following action and inner dialog unfolded in just a few seconds: "I experienced a boom: 'Booom!' I remember feeling it more than hearing it. Then a large fireball! I don't remember specifically thinking 'What's going on right now?' but I'm sure that was what I was thinking.

"When you watch a war movie and you see explosions, you know exactly what it is because you're prepared to experience it . . . you're at a war movie, right? But when you're just doing your job, whatever it may be, and the day seems like any other day, and within moments the mundane is interrupted with 'Boom!' followed by fire and a distant sounding Klaxon, your brain does some gymnastics to make sense of it all.

"Did someone back a truck into the plane? Is a trash truck knocking around a dumpster? Why is there a fireball? Oh, wait . . . I think someone is shelling us! No . . . I'm in Iraq, someone is definitely shelling us! Wow, this is kind of exciting! I might die . . . don't think of that. What do I do? Should I draw my gun? Who would I shoot at? The sky? I'll run over there! Boom! Nope . . . I'll run back to my plane. . . . Boom! You're out in the open, dummy! Get cover! Wait, my crew is back at the plane. I need to run to the plane!" (Sullivan, personal interview, 2018)

That's what a real emergency sounds like. You can't reproduce it, not without provoking Gladys to blow someone's head off. So with that in mind, here are some guidelines for true drill fidelity—without the stage blood.

Before you begin your meat and potatoes, legally mandated school drills, make sure people know what it is that they are actually doing. This will both aid retention and help make the drill less like a meaningless chore that students will shuffle through numbly.

Provide context. Describe the drill to staff and students—tell them what will most likely happen; for instance, in an intruder drill, they will hear an announcement over the public address system that the school is in "lockdown." The school will be in "lockdown" for at least fifteen minutes as administrators, maintenance workers, and safety team designees walk the building, checking that classroom doors are locked.

Again, no partial vesting here. Nobody is going to enjoy being in lockdown for fifteen minutes, but this isn't about winning the popularity contest, and if you tell people what to expect ahead of time, they will handle this duration just fine. Whether it is in a drill or a genuine emergency, people are much happier when they know the score.

For example, when you have people evacuate a school at top speed in a real emergency, the police are not going to let people back into a crime scene to fetch their keys or cell phone. There are accounts of teachers having meltdowns over not being able to go back in and get their keys once the immediate danger is over and it's time for the police to work the night away. However, if they know this is how it goes ahead of time, people become much calmer and more compliant. Any emergency is a surprise, but reducing the nasty little subsurprises that occur along the way makes everyone much easier to handle.

Before the practice drill, explicitly tell people that it is best if they get behind a lockable door. But if this isn't possible, they need to remember the mantra from the top of this book: Embrace, Assess, Inventory, and Decide. That is, recognize and embrace the fact that you are in chaos; assess the context and situation; inventory your options; and make a decision in the best interests of yourself or those under your care. This could include concealment, escaping the school via a proximal door or window, or confronting the intruder if one's life is in direct peril.

Inform people of the date of the drill, but with only an approximate time, such as "before lunch." This prevents people from assuming "crash positions" before the actual drill. Tell staff that they will be emailed a four-question survey at the conclusion of the drill and that they must complete the survey within one hour. Sample questions can include:

a. Where were you during the drill?
b. Did you hear the announcement of the drill?
c. Do you have questions or suggestions?
d. What questions or suggestions did students have?

Compile and share findings with staff within twenty-four hours—either via email or at a staff meeting. You want staff to know that administration read and deliberated over their drill input. Also, it's faster and more effective than checking every door in the school yourself to make sure it can easily be locked in an emergency.

A principal could note the top three concerns of staff and balance that with three things that were not concerns. Then he or she will write an action-able report on what didn't go so well, such as, "It was noted that the public address couldn't be heard in the locker rooms, and two teachers indicated that their doors couldn't be locked." Incorporate this survey into every drill and follow up on the issues noted by staff.

Chapter Thirteen

Other Options

Tabletop Exercises and Focus Groups

But hang on, you're thinking. We can't just neglect to have a plan for at least a good chunk of the possible different scenarios, can we? Firing rubber bullets at kids is extreme. But ignoring the history of the past three decades and just doing fire drills like it's the 1980s . . . that's swinging a bit too far in the opposite direction, isn't it?

For certain. However, you are not faced with a choice between having drills and binders for every conceivable situation and ignoring the range of catastrophes. Shoot for the golden mean. There are plenty of things you can do that fit into the middle ground. Once you've done your basic solid evacuation drills required by law, you can choose from a range of other options for briefing students and staff on an array of possible unpleasant events.

Start with focus groups of six to eight staff or students. This is known as qualitative analysis, and you can align awfully well with the steps of the scientific method, which begins with asking a question. Then you code the answers into groups of similar statements to see where common themes occur.

"Notification," for example, was a concern mentioned by several students at one school. Students were sometimes off campus for work-study programs or to take courses at the nearby community college. If you're one of these students, how would you know that the school was in a lockdown drill other than walking up to the front door of the school to find that nobody buzzes you into the building no matter how many times you pound the button?

Qualitative information gathering, in the form of small focus groups, encourages participants to ask questions and to take the discussion in new directions. The information you gather is important, but you're also getting students to engage with the subject.

These features of the qualitative method are less prevalent in quantitative practices, which aim to generate numerical data. For example, many surveys are passive. They ask the participant to respond to questions such as, "On a scale from one to ten, how safe do you feel at school?" Well, this will provide you with numbers, such as an average of 7.2 for the 150 students who completed the survey, but what does that mean?

And quantitative processes are full of what is called positionality. They represent what one person, or a few people, believe to be the relevant issues. Have you ever filled out a personality quiz and been perplexed because none of the answers fit you? That's positionality.

You also lose the opportunity to clarify the questions. In the earlier example, what does "safe" mean? You might be trying to find out whether students are afraid of intruders, but they answer your question based on their own more pressing concern: the hallway floors are slippery and the playground equipment isn't maintained.

In the safety business these are called "constructs." Constructs might include physical environment safety, feeling safe from weather threats or harm from others, understanding how to identify and report threats, feeling safe on social media, and so on. You develop the constructs first and then develop questions to inform the constructs—but again, this is much more effective in small focus groups, as you'll receive descriptive information from students rather than simply selecting a number between one and ten.

So why aren't safety focus groups common practice in schools? Because they require more time than surveys. Allocation of scarce resources in schools is about priorities—and principals will go for the fast option.

But still, most schools focus on surveys rather than focus groups, partly in an effort to save time and money but also because many safety professionals still think they work.

We were snookered into believing that surveys are terrific tools for figuring out problems (probably due to a generation of leaders that watched too much *Family Feud* as kids or only purchased the toothbrush recommended by four out of five dentists).

There are seven flaws in the practice of using surveys:

Aggregation: Surveys aggregate, or combine, data from many survey takers. For example, one might deduct from collective findings of a youth risk survey of three hundred high school students that "15 percent of youth surveyed had suicidal thoughts at least twice during the past year."

At first glance, this appears like sound, useful information. It isn't. In fact, it's largely useless. Why? Who are the 15 percent of students that have considered suicide? Those 15 percent might all be part of the group that witnessed a particular traumatic event, or it might just be all the freshmen.

Freshman year is rough and hormonal; this doesn't mean your entire student body is 15 percent despondent.

Response rates: How many surveys do you receive that are actually completed? People dislike filling out long forms for no reward. Response rates for emailed surveys might hover at 2 percent. Almost everyone will ignore a survey. And the people who do bother to respond may be doing so because they have some sort of statistically unlikely ax to grind. Survey takers self-select for disgruntled.

Positionality: As I mentioned earlier, the questions center on the point of view of the person(s) writing the questions. The survey will mirror the mind of its author, and that often can lead to bias. I mean, how many human resources directors want to craft a survey that will reveal the true level of disdain simmering within employees? The researcher's own position in relation to the study (in this case, an HR director who really doesn't want to know what anyone thinks of her) skews the data collected and the way in which it is interpreted.

Interpretation: Survey takers are not able to seek clarification of the questions. Surveys are one way and timing is everything! Questions are contextualized to whatever is trending in the media. This is known as the "positive recency effect" and it means that if a school shooting happened yesterday, survey takers would be primed to recite the fears injected into their consciousness by the blaring news media. And a publicized school shooting is the impetus for a hastily built safety survey thrust upon your local school's teachers and students. Measurement will rival the accuracy of an amateur magician flicking playing cards at a top hat.

Constructs: It's not easy to ask "good" questions. Formulating constructs takes thought and clear operational definitions. The most effective surveys have the fewest questions—maybe twenty—and they must pepper construct-aligned questions throughout the survey instead of clumping them into sections.

Jargon: Most surveys are written with industry jargon, so they won't be understood by all survey takers, even college graduates. Then when you add in very young people or youth and adults with disabilities or language barriers, comprehension plummets and you largely end up with people guessing because they simply don't understand the questions. This might even be a form of passive discrimination. Nobody does a readability check on a survey, even though such a task can be accomplished in five minutes with a simple cut-and-paste into free online readability sites.

Generic Data: People generalize survey findings beyond the unit of measure. For example, if you do a survey at a single elementary school and then apply the results to that school, that's much more useful than taking surveys from one hundred elementary schools, combining the findings, and then distilling blanket conclusions. Contexts and situations are lost under such common practices, and the more you aggregate findings the less you represent the "unit of measure."

These are all valid data-related problems with surveys. However, the biggest weakness of surveys is their failure to engage students. Replacing genuine student involvement in safety with surveys is just another way of strengthening the youth code of silence referred to a few chapters earlier.

Students don't care about school safety when feeling they have no control anyway and that the adults are always at the helm. Clearing a path through that code of silence means allowing them to have experiences that expand their torus. They also need to be genuinely involved in safety.

In 2008, the U.S. Secret Service and U.S. Department of Education released a study titled "Prior Knowledge of Potential School-Based Violence: Information Students Learn May Prevent a Targeted Attack." The findings were alarming and suggested that the youth code of silence contributed to most school shootings.

Per the report, "Participants displayed a range in their actions and willingness to come forward. A continuum emerged between bystanders who took no action and those bystanders who were proactive in conveying information related to the threat to others.

"For instance, while some came forward without external prompting and were entirely forthcoming, others revealed the information they knew only after repeated prodding from adults, including school safety officials. In addition, some bystanders did not share their information with anyone or attempt to come forward, while others discussed the information with, or sought the advice of, peers and adults. Information from the Safe School Initiative case files indicated that only 4% of the individuals with prior knowledge attempted to dissuade the attacker from violence" (U.S. Secret Service and U.S. Department of Education, 2008, p. 6).

Chapter Fourteen

What Is a Tabletop Exercise?

A tabletop exercise is when a combination of school staff, police, fire, emergency responders, and even parents meet in an informal setting to talk about their responses.

The reason it's considered a "drill" of sorts is because the specific crisis scenario isn't revealed until you launch the exercise—there's an element of surprise. They are highly valuable in helping people work through potential bomb threats, power outages, bus accidents, and so on. And as a good host, you might offer delicious bagels along with coffee and other refreshments. The entire agenda should take about seventy-five minutes.

Here's some ground to go over with participants before the start of the exercise.

1. The scenario is plausible; events occur as presented.
2. There are no trick questions or hidden agendas.
3. The scenario will run for a determined duration and terminate once time has expired (even if you are in the middle of parsing out an issue).
4. Focus on process, identifying options, and making decisions.
5. Processes will be evaluated following, and not during, the drill. Outcomes will not be evaluated. Therefore, do not feel that your decisions will be judged as right or wrong.
6. Not all answers are known. Unresolved issues that can't be adequately addressed in the moment will be discussed during the "hotwash" that follows the exercise.
7. A designated observer will chronologically log all decisions.
8. Keep the discussion moving—brisk pace.

These exercises help each staff member imaginatively walk through more material in an hour's time than you could get to in a week of drills—and with more engagement of the participants' critical thinking faculties.

Instead of rolling around on the floor pretending to be shot at, tabletop exercises allow groups of ten to twenty people to think through the multiple possibilities that could evolve from any given situation—and to actually practice the thought processes that are required for dealing with these volatile, unpredictable situations in real time.

The facilitator can also introduce spur-of-the-moment injects, or "curveballs," that require people to adjust to the nonlinear unfolding of a crisis. (Think of the dungeon master, if you've ever played *Dungeons and Dragons*.)

Would staff consider physically separating students from their backpacks, or would they simply allow them to exit with them and then search the backpacks after the students were a suitable distance from the structure?

The importance of such injects isn't to try to think of every conceivable variable that might manifest during a crisis—and you have to use them judiciously, as you don't want to bog down the natural flow of the exercise.

But they are great training in getting people to expect nonlinear developments and to quickly evaluate those situations and make decisions. This is also known as teaching situational discretion—and it works. (If you're still wondering, participants decided it was more important to get the students out of the building than to enforce a procedure.)

FEMA offers a free online course titled "IS-0139.a, Exercise Design and Development" that will equip you with the requisite skills for exercise design considerations, exercise objectives, and handling developing scenarios and exercise documentation, which includes a process known as a "hotwash," or immediate "after exercise" discussions and evaluations of participants' or agencies' performance during the tabletop drill (U.S. Federal Emergency Management Agency, 2018).

Note that we want to examine process and not outcomes. This is important as it's not the way people in schools measure things. The teacher's measurement tools are intended to detect students' demonstration of knowledge (convergent) and not exhibition of understanding (divergent). Analysis of the process reveals synthesis, or how different variables, including those participating in the drill, interacted in developing the whole activity of the tabletop exercise.

If we improve process, outcomes will subsequently more closely align to our objectives. When you only look at outcomes, you ignore the heuristics of drills or all the options that were available to participants to help them solve problems. People often are not aware of options; we need to spend time both on the inventory of existing resources and discovery of resources.

A glass of water in the desert has come in the form of a district realizing its phone system can also be configured to send text alerts. People often aren't aware of the tools at their disposal, and this is attributable to accelerating turnover without an induction process—a way to pass the wand of institutional knowledge.

Tabletop exercises improve participants' ability to make judgments quickly and efficiently, and this is apparent with groups that engage in a quarterly exercise as people function in a progressively fluid manner with practice. Regardless of the scenario and injects, they are not constantly stopping to think about their next course of action, something observed in groups' inaugural exercises in which people are nervous, flustered, and critical of self and others.

Again, the exercise facilitator's role includes helping people understand how they became aware of options and by what criteria they whittled down options to make decisions. This method incorporates reflection and introspection, which are more valuable than passing judgment. We spend too much time on outcomes in schools—finger pointing and assigning winners and losers.

Chapter Fifteen

Video Boondoggle

We've taken enough swings at the safety industry for the moment. Just to be fair—well, mostly to cut through another layer of stupid and crazy—let's swing over to laugh at some stupid government tricks. When you read the following initiative, if you think it's a joke, you're not alone.

"So the Department of Homeland Security and the Army got together and decided to make teachers play a video game to help them learn to deal with school shootings."

Yes, fellow taxpayers. We paid for the government to create a first-person shooter game to use in classrooms to try to teach staff how to deal with a real-life shooting. The teacher can play the role of the teacher, a student, or even the shooter . . . in order to . . . who knows, maybe in case they have a meltdown. Or maybe this is directed at getting inside the enemy's head, as though a school shooting were just a really fast chess game in which all the spectators could die (Fox News, 2017).

At first, this might sound reasonable in some ways. The proponents of this training will say it helps educators to make a decision, a choice, during a chaotic event. This reasoning plugs into—but totally misdirects—people's gut instincts about the bagel.

At some level, despite having linear drills shoved down their throats, teachers understand that they need to learn to deal with the totally unexpected. So they go along with it. In reality, like shooter drills with rubber bullets, this is useless. You're not teaching the torus to staff here any more than a virtual trip to Washington, DC, is teaching it to students. Playing a video game is not simulated chaos—if it were, video games would only be popular with psychopaths! The teacher knows it is a game. There's no real danger. They're not dealing with life outside the torus or even overtly learning that it is important to do so. They're just doing yet another classroom exercise.

Another actual fact that developers of these useless games cling to is that video games are indeed a proven, effective way to teach particular skills. In fact, many schools are starting to use the popular game Minecraft® to help elementary students explore math and science concepts.

But safety is not about that kind of precise concept; it depends on a different set of skills. One of them is thinking outside of the bagel. Another is knowing the exact layout of the facility and the most efficient way to move yourself and your students within it—which a government-issued video game is never going to do.

Even if they spent even more money to tailor versions of the game to the layout of every school they distribute it to, you're still not physically navigating the school! These are skills that are taught in basic drills.

So don't be duped by the argument that video games are sound instructional tools and therefore sound *safety* instructional tools. Imagine if after 9/11 the fire department came out with a video game called *Plane Terrorist Attack* that let every middle manager who works in a New York high rise assume the role of passenger, pilot, hijacker, office worker in the building, etc.

No, a lesson of 9/11 was that it makes no sense to have people in high rises drill for plane crashes because it's such a miniscule probability. In NYC there have been a grand total of three buildings hit by planes in the past seventy-five years—and one of them was an accident (the Empire State Building was hit by a military fighter plane in the fog in 1945). And school shootings are in fact very rare—like any disaster, they are much rarer than *emergencies in general*.

Because you can't drill everything, it's far more important to do more general and basic drills. Yet this "training" will be gladly adopted by schools, and that very rareness will make it impossible to measure their effectiveness.

Did it make the staff more prepared for an active shooter? Who knows? Only 0.0000001 percent of the schools that used the video had a shooting, and every one of those was completely different from the circumstances of previous shootings on which they built the game.

What a boondoggle. A well-designed tabletop exercise and a discussion with staff about "here's what to expect during a crisis" would be miles more valuable than having the teacher take the controller and "shoot the bad guy." And once again, this kind of drill is uselessly linear by definition; video games lead the player down the garden path, offering nothing random and no ability to simulate the real-life decision-making process.

This also seems to be an instance in which the government forgot that it already had a well-regarded no-cost FEMA course released on December 28, 2015, titled "Active Shooter: What You Can Do" (U.S. Federal Emergency

Management Agency, 2015). The course has an easy-to-use interface and follows well-designed instructional objectives. But onto the arcade version.

There are constructive ways to use computers to help with shootings by the way. Most students who do shoot actually post their intentions on social media ahead of time. Instead of using computer games to train teachers to deal with specific situations that have already occurred and probably will never reoccur, how about we develop technology to detect threats through social media? And then prepare for the unpredictable!

The kid could be talking about how he's going to kill everyone in school, so you do yet another shooter drill . . . and then he shows up in his mom's SUV and drives over kids at recess instead. If you train the teachers to have good situational awareness instead of knowing exactly how a single shooter in a video game might feel, they're going to do a much better job of reacting and safeguarding the students.

Professor Seann Dikkers is an expert in video games, among other things, and he agreed to an interview about this training tool. Dr. Dikkers has worked in the field of digital pedagogy for more than ten years and served as a middle school teacher and principal for fourteen years prior.

He has published a number of books and articles on the use of video and mobile media games for learning. For any video simulation that is meant as a training, the audience is an essential consideration.

Dikkers says this game's "apparent purpose is to train security and military personnel by presenting them with realistic and repeatable simulations so they can learn to think and make excellent decisions under pressure," adding that such simulations *are* effective in training for military audiences and security personnel, especially when they allow for practicing various scenarios. Debriefing after making mistakes helps people to make better decisions under pressure.

"Under pressure we want that training to 'take over' and help desensitize soldiers to elements they have already processed cognitively because they have seen them in the simulations. Simulations then help with speed, accuracy, decision making, and can minimize real trauma by exposure to fake trauma. So this kind of tool could help first responders save lives."

However, for an audience of teachers, who have no base training in combat situations, the takeaway is greatly reduced. "Do we need large numbers of people exposed to fake trauma when the likelihood of real trauma is minimal?" When the audience is school administrators and personnel, the reasons for using the simulation are largely removed.

Further, he notes that there have apparently not been any cost/benefit analyses done to see if this training has any benefit or if it is worth the time teachers will spend on it. Time out of class must be spent wisely and could be spent doing a training that actually applies to teaching, which is what they will in fact do for most of their careers.

When safety training is done, it should be applied to the basic survival skills that will actually be far more useful in the vast majority of disasters that will occur. Once again, any particular disaster is rare; time is better spent on general torus training and basic disaster-specific skills, such as running from a shooter on a diagonal and throwing things at the shooter's face if you can't run or hide.

The benefits of anything they will learn in an overly specific shooter simulation that doesn't even involve physical training are minimal. Taking five minutes to drive home three basic skills—zigzag away, run, and throw things—is worth more than three hours of playing a simulation game.

Most important, Dikkers asks us to take a step back from the mechanics of trying to prevent a shooting while it is in progress from killing everyone in the room and focus on preventing a shooting before it ever starts. Because who are the vast majority of school shooters? That's right, they're unhappy students. He notes that specific shootings are hard to train for because the events always unfold differently, but there is always "one common variable": "a shooter that is disconnected and sociopathic enough to kill. This is often detectable in community and preventable with treatment. Post-tragedy interviews often tell a tragic tale of a community that saw a number of warning signs, even correctly sought help, yet didn't take measures to intervene, work with parents, or even search a bedroom for weapons."

Rather than spending hours having teachers play simulations in which they try to kill a student who has turned on everyone, why not spend those hours teaching staff to make better connections with those students before they turn to desperate acts?

Dikkers states, "If the basics of crisis safety are simple to teach, I would advocate we put the vast majority of our time into training and simulations that show teachers and administration methods to connect with students, build mentoring relationships with them, and how to recruit students into extra-curricular activities (including gamer clubs)."

Instead of a shooting situation, Dikkers jokingly suggests "a Diner Dash like game for classroom management and touching base with kids on a cyclical rotation"—in other words, training teachers to move around the room to give attention to and learn about every student. "Our goal should be to show care to every student, every day. Prevention is better than crisis management. The cost would be similar and the benefits touch every student-teacher relationship. . . . Let's focus on relationships that remove the motivations to kill. Let's spend five million on that!" (Dikkers, personal interview, 2018).

Chapter Sixteen

One More Don't

Professional Standards for Educational Leaders

Here's one more complaint when it comes to drills and safety: the entire text of the National Policy Board for Educational Administration *Professional Standards for Educational Leaders* (PSEL) (2015). This document, created by the Council of Chief State School officers in 2015, replaced the 1996 and 2008 versions of the ISLLC (Interstate School Leaders Licensure Consortium) guidelines, which were already terrible.

You guys can get this wrong once, but three times? Changing the name of the ill-conceived document and shuffling a few sentences around hasn't fooled anyone. Come on.

What is the PSEL? These are the educational training standards that our university education programs teach to future school leaders and teachers, and they are a complete and unadulterated mess when it comes to school safety. Our professional standards have missed the boat. They are escapist fantasies that provide a psychological flight to a utopian classroom.

What's the cause of the mess? It's seldom the faculty; the standards themselves are pillow stuffing. Universities are bringing more and more adjunct faculty on board. In educational leadership, this is a good thing, as you're more likely to be taught by someone from the trenches than someone from the ivory tower. The part-time folks who delivered from the field shared invaluable firsthand accounts and resources.

But then you have your full timers, your tenured cases. These ivory tower folks might have taught years ago, and a few retained their edge, but others became insulated and soft and love to hold forth about motivation, effective leadership, and whatever other drivel they wrote about in the books they conveniently sold as required course readings. Put them out in the cold for thirty minutes and they would stand there and freeze.

The problem with educational administration programs at the postsecondary level, or to be delivered to on-the-job administrators, is that the standards for such programs are cast in foam. Many air pockets for echo chambers, flexible enough for interpretation to pretty much any circumstance, and they might feel good to stand on or touch, but they aren't foundations you can build on.

In the mold of its 2008 predecessor, this hot mess was developed as a collaborative effort by countless organizations and contributors. (Of the thirty-six-page document they released in 2015, 20 percent of the real estate is allocated to acknowledging contributors to the document. Perhaps there's an accompanying applause track if available in audio format.)

This document has failed to say anything serious about school safety in a time when school safety is every other headline on the news and school safety bills litter the floors of Congress. It is a wash of meaningless weasel words, meant to slither through its paces while mollifying every potential complainant who might look at it with an eye to his or her political bêtes noires rather than actual safety. The NPBEA document, used by at least forty-five states and the District of Columbia, makes this boast about its guideposts. It claims that they are "grounded in current research and the real-life experiences of educational leaders, they articulate the leadership that our schools need and our students deserve. They are student-centric, outlining foundational principles of leadership to guide the practice of educational leaders so they can move the needle on student learning and achieve more equitable outcomes. They're designed to ensure that educational leaders are ready to meet effectively the challenges and opportunities of the job today and in the future as education, schools and society continue to transform" (p. 7).

Do you need a cup of coffee now? This could have been written by an algorithm. To use more words to say nothing, you would have to be working for a state senator or designing a new version of *lorem ipsum*.

The guide also states: "The Standards are foundational to all levels of educational leadership. They apply to principals and assistant principals and they apply to district leaders as they engage in similar domains of work as school leaders. However, the specific leadership activities that follow each Standard are cast more toward school-level leadership than district-level leadership. Moreover, district-level leaders have additional responsibilities associated with their particular roles (e.g., working with school boards and labor relations), and those responsibilities extend beyond these Standards. Such additional responsibilities are described in other standards focusing specifically on district-level leadership" (p. 8).

In other words, they've written a document that applies to the entire profession. Congratulations, that's your basic job. The actual standards, however, are uselessly broad, a shameful exercise in flowery, subjective, idealistic language that makes the document not incomplete but useless. Trying to follow this garbage would make it harder to safeguard your school, not easier.

The words "safety," "violence," "security," and "threat" did not appear in the document. The word "safe" appeared in the following contexts: "As shown in Figure 1 on page 5, at the core, students learn when educational leaders foster safe, caring and supportive school learning communities and promote rigorous curricula, instructional and assessment systems" (p. 10). Not a word about how to *actually foster anything safe*.

"Build and maintain a safe, caring, and healthy school environment that meets that [*sic*] the academic, social, emotional, and physical needs of each student" (p. 13). Once again, no advice.

"Safeguard and promote the values of democracy, individual freedom and responsibility, equity, social justice, community and diversity" (p. 16). Sigh. Once again, no concrete advice, but at least they don't have to be accountable if anything goes wrong.

Insofar as anyone in the profession will pay attention to this sludge, it will only serve to distract and impede, wasting everyone's scant time and offering no evidence for anything (not that you could prove anything about "fostering" an environment to begin with). It's embarrassing. With all the staff and resources they had on hand, they lost out on a huge opportunity to create something that would be useful. What they did was worse than not doing anything at all.

Some may argue that the document is not a curriculum and that training programs must be able to tailor courses to the contexts and situations of the aspiring administrators that they serve and specific state mandates and local policies and blah, blah.

By that logic, it's useless in every educational capacity for which it claims to be a beacon. It's these types of feel good, collectivist missives that distract educators from the real work at their feet.

There is no excuse for conveniently side-stepping school safety in this document. None at all. You can't even use the explanation that this was your first time at the plate. It's unfathomable to think that not one reviewer of this document questioned the absenteeism.

Hey, you want to remain a mile wide and an inch deep, you could have done that by at the very least establishing criteria for checking that educational leaders are aware of the safety resources afforded to them by federal and state governments (such as those free school safety training modules from the FEMA) or helping them understand how to teach students to identify and report threats of harm to self or others.

Part IV

Systems Will Develop, So Let Them

Chapter Seventeen

The Zen of Safety

By now, you have probably noticed that as much as we would love for it to be straightforward—as devoutly as we wish sheer force of will, goodwill, and cash could keep people safe—the science of building safety systems and training people to be safe is never going to be exact. As unpleasant as this fact may be, it has to be dealt with. This is another facet of the paradoxes of chaos: as much as you would like to plan a system, a procedure, and a very specific protocol for disasters, each individual disaster has a different dynamic, so every instance will have to generate its own system for dealing with the bagel dough that's splattered all over the walls.

Also, as an educator, any decision-making power over that system is unlikely to be in your hands. School employees tend to get used to being in a position of authority—over the students, at least. In a disaster, part of being outside your torus is giving up control both to outside agencies and to the flow of events, which tends to surprise everyone involved, even the people who set them in motion.

The changing dynamics of an event catch the shooters off guard almost as much as they do the victims and bystanders. Even if you're the shooter, and you know when and where and how it's going to begin, everything you've planned begins to fall apart the moment you've fired the first round. So even the intruders are forced to deal with a nonlinear situation—which is a good thing, as they'll be forced to act in ways they didn't predict. Knowing this ahead of time can also be an ace in your pocket.

Letting go is difficult for us, cognitively, as human beings. We don't want to die or see our kids die, however, so we have to work with reality as it comes. Lucky for us, another lesson from Lower Manhattan reassures us that the systems we need *will develop.*

The system rarely matches up one to one with anything any official had planned, so once again general prep will always outperform specific drills. This chapter will show how you can improve the system that develops in your school or jurisdiction.

It should not surprise you that the answer is another paradox. The systems will develop on their own and run until everyone runs out of adrenaline, but the quality and effectiveness of the systems vary from one crisis to another.

The two main variables controlling the system's performance are (1) the whims of that day's circumstances (for instance, 9/11 happened under excellent weather conditions for sailing) and (2) the prep work you put into getting people ready to form those systems (for instance, the way the rescuees' expectations dovetailed with the arrival of the impromptu fleet).

The former is largely out of your control, with the exception of any infrastructure you can control—say, fire exit design. The second is something you can do something about. As this book keeps shouting at you, part of that is teaching the torus. Another part is taking advantage of transference. The final part is knowing how systems in general work in crisis, examining the circumstances of your school or facility, and improving people's ability to feed into those systems.

That sounds horribly abstract, but there are concrete principles and goals to work with. You can hit it from several angles: increase your staff's knowledge of the institution and facility but, just as important, train everyone to know that a system will develop and that their job is to help it develop rather than hinder it. As with the torus, increasing people's awareness of the forces at work is half the battle. But first, you need to understand the general principles yourself.

Similarly, we have other technological and knowledge improvements at our fingertips that have developed since 9/11 that could improve our crisis response—if we know how to use them.

Chapter Eighteen

Incident Command Structure

Before we hit the psychological phenomena, let's check out a little tech example. On 9/11, the maritime rescuers were operating on a totally different communication channel from the official emergency crews. The fleet members were using maritime radio, which is a bit like the trucker CB radios of the *Smokey and the Bandit* era. The rest of the crews, like the firefighters, were using Incident Command Structure (ICS). ICS is a phrase that sounds intrinsically boring.

But read on because the September 11 attacks and ICS offer a great example of how systems self-tailor during a crisis—and how even within the same crisis, different aspects of the battle will respond better to one type of system than another aspect will. This is also a puzzling story due to the fact that ICS pretty much disintegrated on 9/11.

Not that seeing ICS disintegrate was all that strange considering the tech they had available at the time, especially when it came to cell phone towers and batteries. If you're forty or older you probably think that battery cells in the 1990s were perfectly fine. You'd be surprised how primitive they were compared to what we have now, Gramps!

Here's a little background on ICS. The name "Incident Command Structure" sounds like a permanent hierarchical system. But although it creates a temporary hierarchy of command, the name is mostly a convoluted way of calling it a communication protocol. When personnel arrive on scene, we say they're "setting up an ICS." They are using a preset language structure and the personnel on hand to set up a temporary chain of command for that event.

Firefighters started the ICS back in the 1970s. There had been a number of failures in the firefighting and emergency response system, and everybody blamed it on things like lack of manpower, equipment, or water . . . until they figured out the problems were occurring because their communications were a confusing mess. Instead of using English words across communications channels to send information and commands to colleagues, they were using codes, like "10-23!"

Not only was this counterintuitive with a difficult learning curve, using numbers rather than words made it harder to piece together what someone was saying from context if they were broken up by radio static—which, back then, happened more often than not. Worse, if more than one department had to work together, they often used different codes and found coordination impossible.

They wanted to make things both consistent and easy to understand, which meant using plain language—but in a coded form. That means that when you show up to a theater of action, you don't radio in a non-English code like "10-23," but nor do you freestyle: "Hey, so uh, I'm at the uh thingie, what do I do now?" Instead, everybody says "on scene," and everyone knows what that means.

In the 1980s and onward, ICS was expanded to police, EMS (ambulance), and other emergency responders. ICS makes sure that all available resources are accounted for and spread across all of the jurisdictions that are affected by a crisis; ideally, if there's a wildfire in California, for example, you don't get all the firefighters stuck in one quadrant because one county doesn't want to coordinate with the next.

ICS works well if it is properly applied, which can best be done in slower-developing, large-scale incidents, like that wildfire. But if you are responding to a quick "holy crud" event like a school shooting—when the bagel has fallen apart instantly—the seams begin to show. The first police officer or officers will enter the building quickly because they have to. They don't wait to set up an ICS; that happens later. So the first few hours—which sometimes means the entire crisis—can be chaos.

For instance, during the Columbine school massacre, the responders' attempts at ICS were a mess. There were multiple SWAT teams inside of the school at the same time, and most of them had no idea where the others were.

Responders were uncertain as to who was in charge of the scene—was it the local law enforcement, Denver SWAT unit, or some other agency? It doesn't help that, compared to firefighters, police tend to operate by objectives and are loners ("I'm off to accomplish X; you go over there and do Y"). Firefighters are more dependent on teamwork.

The communication system is far from perfect too. It's a huge improvement in clarity and ease of comprehension over every department having their own number codes; there was a good deal of improvement, both in the language we used—using words instead of numbers usually helps, unless your organization is multilingual or international in scope—and in the technology.

And yet the key words are still not always totally intuitive or easy to distinguish from one another. In short, ICS emerged, but hasn't evolved. It is what it is: a clear leader and plain language.

But there's a catch. Radio communications expert Fred Varian points out a nugget of trouble. (Mr. Varian has been both an active amateur radio operator and a telecommunications pro since 1964; he also has twenty years of experience as a firefighter/EMS first responder, and he combines all this knowledge to provide unique insight into communications operations, security, and intelligence.)

Varian says most Incident Command Management programs choose to encrypt digital radio communications, so they can reduce the opportunity for messages to be picked up by civilian radio scanners.

This means we take all those nice, clear verbal messages and scramble the signal so that only those who are supposed to hear the message can hear the message. He notes that encryption is done for reasons of communication security (ComSec) and per what are known as ComSec protocols, which restrict sharing confidential information. This makes sense in that you don't want the public, and possibly the perpetrator, listening to police communications during a school intruder situation.

Unfortunately, it also can wreak havoc on interagency communication. As Fred states, "There is a downside to using encryption on all the [radio] channels for all traffic. In case of a disaster where mutual aid from other groups is needed, communications inter-operability is much more difficult" (Varian, 2013).

The limitations and vulnerabilities of ICS were even more clearly exposed when the World Trade Center towers fell. Fire and law enforcement radios were not fully compatible; radios had limited range and were hampered by barriers such as tall buildings and limited battery life. Radios at that time were transitioning from analog to digital, so it was like having a house in 2009 with new digital flat-screen TVs and a few bulkier, grainier analog cathode ray tube TVs.

With unreliable radio communications, responders switched to secondary means such as cellular phones. As soon as they tried the phones, however, they found that the New York City cellular network was quickly overwhelmed with so many attempted calls—from emergency workers, civilians, victims, worried relatives, and pretty much the entire population of the city. Worse, all this traffic flooded into key communication cables that were physically damaged by the wreckage.

Welcome to the firefighters' world on 9/11! Not only were they rushing into a collapsing high rise to save people, they couldn't communicate. Meanwhile, the harbor rescuers were having a much easier time using maritime radio. The onboard units were not reliant on the small battery packs that are practical for use with handheld radios, and out on the water they were not getting interference from tall buildings, nor is maritime radio dependent on cable infrastructure. The harbor fleet was therefore working with the advantage of having a more flexible power structure.

Modern communication systems are substantially more robust and redundant than their 2001 counterparts. ICS has been embedded into training for emergency responders and even utility companies, hospitals, and less formal rescue organizations such as Cajun Navy Relief. It is highly unlikely that radio interoperability and cellular tower capacities would indirectly succumb to an act of terrorism.

Communication platforms and subsequently ICS would be preserved during future sentinel incidents, as successfully stress tested by the Boston Marathon bombing in 2013 and Hurricanes Harvey and Irma in 2017. Terrorists would have to take out a cluster of cell towers to really compromise service.

Fascinating, you're thinking, but what's the lesson here for schools? According to safety expert Timothy Riecker, ICS works for departments that use it often. But as it is so complex, it's not for everyone—especially those in professions in which people didn't sign up to be first responders.

But some cities push it on them anyway. Riecker (2018) uses the example of an apartment manager being pushed to use ICS. Even if you send that manager through training, because he or she isn't likely to use it in the next twelve months (or five years, really), he or she isn't going to retain something that complex for that long without using it.

For non-first-responder professionals like the apartment manager, as well as the amateur boat captains who helped out on 9/11—or, more to the point here, teachers!—a complex professional system like ICS is not something we should try to rope them into. Instead, once again they should be trained more generally in thinking about their torus, situational awareness, and the ability to go with systems that develop organically in a crisis.

This means that instead of teaching teachers ICS, we need to teach them to trust their own instincts and stop looking for specific directives at every turn. We need to give teachers more personal initiative and fewer on-high directives—or at least train them to understand that their main on-high directive is to trust their own instincts!

However, as Riecker also wisely specifies, each school does need to have at least one point of contact person who knows what he or she is doing with ICS to enough of a degree to be able to coordinate with responders in a crisis. If you want to be that person or appoint that person, there are plenty of resources for training. The Federal Emergency Management Agency (FEMA) operates a Preparedness Branch that includes the Emergency Management Institute (EMI). EMI offers good, free online courses in several areas of emergency management.

The most important thing you should know, however, is that as an educator you will never know ICS in-depth the way responders do.

So even if you ace the course, keep in mind that you won't be in charge if there's a crisis at your school that warrants an ICS response. Yes, the system staggered on 9/11, but that's because it was not as firmly backed by tech as it is now. It went down due to failure of the communication structure, radio batteries, and signal strength.

However, those issues are resolved in 2018; now understanding ICS is crucial, if only so you're aware that you need to get out of the way. Your main job as point person will be to ask, "Who is the incident commander?" and then follow his or her instructions; you take the training in order to be able to *understand* their instructions, not to override them.

Remember, no matter how well you teach the bagel to yourself and your students, it's this person's job to live in chaos. The incident commander will tell you what he or she needs from you and your staff during the crisis and will stand beside you during press updates. You also need to know that the incident commander role may change hands; the first cops to get to the school will take over, and one of them will become the ICS commander, but as more police arrive, that role may well be transferred to a higher-ranking person. Just go with the flow.

With that being said, there remain serious drawbacks to ICS that you still need to contend with today. As you won't be the incident commander, there may not be a lot you can do about them, but as with anything else, being aware of them in detail will help you make decisions when the time comes; any information you have will be a help, although barely ever in a predictable way.

So let's dive in. First, fire and EMS will rarely enter a perimeter until it has been determined "cleared" by police. So even though we may do inter-agency drills, in real life, coordination doesn't tend to occur so smoothly. During the Virginia Tech shooting in 2007, fire and EMS staged blocks away from the action and wouldn't come to Norris Hall for a couple of hours because they wanted confirmation from police that there were no other threats in the building. Police actually used their SUVs to shuttle victims to the location of staged medical teams. (The SUVs were so contaminated with bodily fluids that they were permanently removed from service.)

This also happened at the Sikh temple shooting in Oak Creek, Wisconsin, in 2012: fire and EMS waited on the road for several minutes until police determined the site to be secure. This almost cost a wounded officer his life because EMS wouldn't go to him until their superiors had an all clear from the police.

But before the police would give the all clear, they in turn had to follow their own procedures, which means they had to search all the nooks and crannies of the place of worship, from the building to the shrubs and cars in the parking lot.

Another twist to the Sikh temple incident was that many worshipers placed frantic calls to their relatives in India. As a result, some of the relatives placed calls back to the local authorities to seemingly inform them of the shooting.

So there was this vicious, slightly delayed communication loop that made it seem that there were additional shootings unfolding. You can just imagine the frenetic exchanges of those phone calls. It took several minutes to dampen this feedback loop and for authorities to recognize what was happening with the incoming calls from India.

If it is an active shooter, fire and EMS wait for police to sweep the scene, and this can take an hour or longer. There are a lot of rooms in even a mid-sized school. You also get literally hundreds of police, fire, and EMS, on and off duty, responding to these big calls. Trying to manage them can be almost impossible—as was the case with the Sikh temple shooting in which adjacent parking lots were packed with responding vehicles and command vehicles to a density that would rival game day tailgating. And it's not *your* job to manage them, it is the job of law enforcement to inventory, stage, and deploy resources.

If you're a school leader, you need to find out as soon as possible who the ICS commander is. There could literally be hundreds of responders on the scene. Better yet, that number could include some personnel that aren't even legit—as happened at 9/11.

During 9/11, Lower Manhattan was quickly closed off—and that helped prevent concerned relatives looking for loved ones as well as responders from flooding the area. EMS, fire, and police will always claim that they work seamlessly in an emergency, but it depends. This claim is truer for a fire or car accident than an active shooter; police don't need to sweep the scene of a car accident, so there's no delay.

But in a situation that is caused by hostile actors, the police are required to make sure everything is clear before anyone else can begin. Tactical fire and tactical EMS teams are in their infancy; while these teams sound good, in practice, a cop is a cop and a firefighter is a firefighter.

Tactical interdisciplinary rescue response is being oversold to the public, particularly for schools served by volunteer firefighters and EMS—which are the majority of schools in the United States. Active shooter environments will remain the jurisdiction of law enforcement. You aren't going to have a team of firefighters in bulletproof turnout coats rushing into a school on the heels of police officers.

Chapter Nineteen

Tornadoes, Hurricanes, and the Fabulous Cajun Navy Relief

On May 22, 2011, a monstrous tornado ripped through the heart of Joplin, Missouri, devastating the majority of homes and businesses in this community of fifty thousand people. It was an EF-5—that's as high as the tornado scale goes. The worst. The fire stations were hit too, and it took several hours for firefighters and responders to reach critical structures, including St. John's Hospital.

Unexpected civilians were quicker to replace what had been shattered: within two hours of the storm strike, mother-daughter duo Rebecca and Genevieve Williams (2012) had founded Joplin Tornado Information (JTI) with an iPhone. (Within two hours as well, some city workers made a unique domain and a crude site to get out information to people—and then worked nonstop for a week updating it.)

But that was one way, whereas JTI was interactive. It began as a Facebook page, but the Williamses pieced in other social networks until the town was more or less tied back together. JTI and its affiliates were staffed entirely by volunteers and accepted no donations.

Another great example of rapid system development came around six years later, during Hurricanes Irma and Harvey in the U.S. southeast.

A system called the Cajun Navy Relief self-organized from groups of locals who had learned the hard way that they couldn't sit and wait for the U.S. government to rescue them. The Cajun Navy Relief formed in 2005 as a response to Hurricane Katrina, during which the government completely broke down, from the feds to the local level, making a disaster into an infamous horror show (Cajun Navy is a broad term to refer to ad hoc rescuers with a range of affiliations).

Katrina seems to have been an example when transference, and trusting in the U.S. government, may have been a rather large mistake. So a grassroots citizen group loosely assembled, with boats, pickups, and supplies to conduct house-to-house rescues.

The Cajun Navy Relief operates with a quiet endorsement from politicians (or at least they don't interfere) and open endorsement from the public. Cajun Navy Relief is funded by donations and the wallets of its members.

During Harvey, it responded to the greater Houston area with boats, trucks, water, food, and personnel of various backgrounds, from farmers to meteorologists, living up to its motto: "We don't wait for help—we are the help." They also took advantage of the latest technology, an app called Zello Walkie Talkie, along with Facebook.

We need to pause and understand the simple linear regressive relationship between social contract theory and the surrendering of personal rights for protection by the state. Had the pendulum of the Patriot Act swung further following September 11, 2001, civilian rescue forces (aiding adults and children) might have been banned per the argument that because they weren't regulated by the state they might pose a threat to national security

One of the organic leaders of the Cajun Navy Relief was Katie Pechon, administration and public information officer. She and others manned the posts and coordinated the rescue of thousands from the seat of their pants. Her first involvement with the Cajun Navy Relief was responding to a Facebook post asking for a forklift, and she collaborated with a relative to try to fulfill that request. She was then thrown into dispatch, then supply, and then, per her account, overnight she was coordinating boat rescues. She was new to the role, having just downloaded the app Zello, and had no training.

Her first boat rescue was a lady surrounded by rising waters at St. Stephen's Catholic Church who contacted her via Facebook Messenger. Katie then sent a Zello request that she needed a boat to go to the church to rescue the lady and her husband. A volunteer with a boat responded—and that was the beginning of pairing hundreds of boats with thousands of victims in a system that literally developed in minutes, scaled, sustained, and then evolved from rescue to recovery as Cajun Navy Relief members, Katie included, helped people gut their homes of water-damaged drywall.

By this time, social media was an even more widespread tool than it had been in Joplin. Pechon and the Cajun Navy Relief made heavy use of Facebook Messenger and the phone app Zello, which was founded in 2011 and had only fourteen employees at the time of the hurricanes, to rescue thousands of people who chose to seek help via social media rather than depending on the traditional 911 system; there was a clear transference dynamic at work, but its object was no longer the government.

More evidence that systems will emerge—and they will also rapidly scale and adapt to the situation. Katie had never been trained in Incident Command

Systems. Yet she interfaced with local emergency responders and governments to assemble collaborative rescues, secure warehouse space to store supplies, and deal with other injects.

Cajun Navy Relief is a perplexing animal when studied through the traditional systems theory lens. Similar to the September 11, 2001, harbor rescue, researchers have a hard time explaining why these "parts" fit together and perform as if engineered from the ground up to be an integrated rescue system.

There seems to be a quantum leap in tech possibilities every few years now—or, better yet, a leap in tech adaptation by civilians. According to Pechon, 2011 was about the point where we transitioned from people going to the Internet for info during a crisis to people using the Internet as the number one tool to obtain help and to communicate with responders, be it preexisting systems like the fire and police squads or spontaneous systems like the Cajun Navy Relief (Pechon, 2017).

By the hurricanes of 2017, drones were added to the mix, albeit in a limited capacity due to capabilities and regulations. Drones were inconsistently regulated across federal, state, and local jurisdictions and the role of volunteer drone rescue individuals or organizations has yet to be quantified or formalized.

For example, in some places it was illegal to fly a drone in a park, but it was okay to stand outside of the park and fly the drone above the park—quirky stuff like that that plays catch-up with new technologies. Also, drones can't operate in high wind, so they had to wait out the hurricane-spawned storms. Drone manufacturers are already testing next-generation models that can operate in adverse weather conditions.

When the weather finally relented, a crude fleet of commercial drones were able to go out to do a rapid inventory of the damaged areas in Texas and Florida. They had to be directed separately because no software was available that was capable of coordinating individual commercial drones into a swarm with a single directive, but the possibilities were exciting.

This was the first large-scale deployment of commercial drones in a disaster and they were already bringing back useful intel. What would be possible if you could send out a swarm of drones honed to converge on a mission? We will find out soon: the U.S. military is currently testing large-scale microdrone swarms, and the technology will be available to commercial drone pilots and local governments within five years. Most fire departments already have at least one drone to survey a scene or engage in search and rescue—something unimaginable in 2001.

Chapter Twenty

Seeing Faces on the Moon

How Pareidolia Helped the Rescue System on 9/11 Develop

So we have seen in the previous few chapters that systems will develop and that you should let them. But to fully make use of this fact, you need to know why this happens.

There are a few psychological and sociological phenomena—most of which are related, at least tangentially, to transference or the torus—that do a good job of explaining the finer points of why systems develop among groups of people who are exposed to a massive, common threat. The first we will look at is pareidolia, a very difficult to spell word that is closely related to transference.

Anglo-Saxon (simpler, but wordy) terminology for pareidolia is "seeing things that aren't there, although the pattern is close enough that we can forgive you." Pareidolia most famously happens with patterns that vaguely resemble faces; if a couple of splotches can be resolved into a face, even if it's a stretch, our brains will do it.

The Man in the Moon meme is classic face pareidolia, for example. It's the result of generations of people looking up at that randomly mottled disc in the sky and thinking, "Well, those kind of look like eyes and a mouth." Obviously the Sea of Tranquility is just a crater in a dead rock, but we want to make out the pattern nonetheless.

This is another strange efficiency that is built into our operating systems. Just as we tend to see our surroundings through filters so we aren't overcome by noise, humans are programmed to resolve random shapes into something we can make sense of.

The link to transference is obvious: no one imagines an object they have never seen projected on the moon, nor do we tend to see things that have made no impression on us. If people are accustomed to seeing a pattern resolve into a certain configuration or event, or if they have been led to expect such a thing, then they will begin to make it out long before it is completely logical to do so. If we expect the authorities to take care of us, then any promising signs will be interpreted as a rescue event. And sometimes pareidolia happens by chance to coincide with reality.

This is another reason why the rescuees who made their way to Battery Park stayed calm and kept moving in the correct direction: they began to see the rescue ships on the horizon. And what they saw in the pattern of ships coming near the harbor was a fleet of ships sent to save them.

Those ships could have been part of several other events: terrorists who had seized local ships and were coming in for another attack; random boaters who were holding an event together, blissfully unaware of the disaster onshore, and heading back in to shore; boaters fleeing yet another attack in New Jersey; captains who were terrified of what might be out on the water and were putting in to shore.

Despite all these possibilities, when the Manhattanites in Battery Park saw this motley collection of vessels come forward, they "observed" what they expected to see: they made out the image of a rescue force, an image prepatterned in their minds by the transference dynamic. They were *primed to think that any cluster of boats was a rescue force.* A day earlier, that same cluster of boats would have been passively dismissed as "harbor boats" doing their "harbor things" . . . ho hum, back to my bagel.

But in an emergency situation, what they saw happened to coincide with a changed reality: they needed badly to be rescued, and look, society had coughed up some kind of rescue effort. Never mind that they aren't uniform, that the first one to come near is a private midlife crisis yacht with a goofy name spray-painted across the bow. They're coming for us! This coincidence of pareidolia with reality made the rescue that much more orderly by providing the rescuees with reassurance and a clear (to them) cue as to where they should go in order to be removed from harm's way.

Chapter Twenty-One

Transitioning into Chaos

*How Increasing the "Noise" Increases Options . . .
Up to a Point*

Generally, people are able to process maybe two or three uncertainties at a time.

For those in Lower Manhattan on 9/11, everything was uncertain. It is essential to remember that the attack was not perceived as "over" after the collapse of Tower 2.

We know now that it was, but for anyone who assumed the worst was over when the first plane struck, all certainty was swept off the table with the impact of the second. Would there be more planes? Was the harbor mined or boats laden with explosives? How about the bridges? God help us, did they have military jets? There was so much happening and so much that could have happened as well.

Along with the sights and sounds of that day, this added up to too many sensory and thought cues for anyone to process. Even on an ordinary day, particularly in a perpetually active city like New York, people are confronted with too many cues to keep up with everything.

People can override the most powerful environmental cues—explosions, alarms, and flaming debris passing a window. Remember the strange talent for focus that was shown by the WTC employees who paused to save their work on their computers as the building collapsed? This is the same talent for concentrating during chaos that directed Admiral Loy and the fleet—focused in the wrong direction.

To take another famous example: for more than an hour after impact, many people refused to believe that the mortally damaged *Titanic* would sink. Even when it broke in two, some passengers believed that the stern, which briefly assumed a horizontal position, would remain afloat.

You truly are a snowflake: everyone has their own pattern of impulses when it comes to dealing with chaos.

Some people are wired to deny it until they can't do anything about it. This is embodied by a scene in the 1983 movie *The Day After*, in which a mother frantically attends to tidying her house as her husband is yelling for her to get into the cellar due to incoming nuclear missiles. She has refused to exit her torus as the horrific image of the pending chaos has overwhelmed her capacity for rational thought.

The magnitude of the phenomena of the 9/11 Twin Tower attacks was so huge that even the most stolid eventually admitted, "Hey, I'm not going to Starbucks this morning." But those most able to survive were those who mentally threw out their plans the minute they heard the crash. The people who did well on 9/11 are the people who immediately realized that today's plan, agenda, and schedule were gone.

A subtler version of this phenomenon (according to Paul Rapp) happens at airports when there are delays. Some people freak out and don't know what to do besides rail and complain. Other people gradually realize that if they sit and wait, they will miss appointments, family events, the concert they were traveling to see . . . or if they're going home, the catsitter needs to be rescheduled and the dry cleaning has to wait another day to be picked up. What are your options? Do not lock into a local decision. Chaos liberates you from conventionalities of behavior. Take a different flight and visit a different city and work your way to your destination from there. That's the heuristic. Inject noise.

Another example is Apollo 13. Within moments, flight command said, "Okay, we aren't going to the moon, we have to construct an alternative flight plan. We have to work the problem." At a fairly high level of chaos, the plan has to go out the window. We can see this as terrifying or we can choose to see it as a chance to pick a new, crazy option if we want to stay alive. Fun?

However, at an even higher level of chaos—a state that rarely lasts for long—the opposite happens: all of your choices are pretty much eliminated except for "freeze and die" or "run away from the collapsing building." This, too, can be liberating; instead of being freed to make new choices, this level of chaos frees you from having to make any choices at all. Run that way.

This is another lesson that was clearly illustrated by the harbor rescue on 9/11: people walked toward the fleet because of pareidolia, but they walked to the park in the first place because they had no other options—they had to go to the harbor if they wanted to get off the island because the roads and bridges were closed. It's counterintuitive, but the more chaos, the better—as your decisions become few and obvious, they become swift and sure.

More improvisation. And under the circumstances, it worked. Under less-than-chaotic conditions, if burning building parts were falling from the sky, you would think twice before letting someone pass you overhead, across a makeshift gangplank, and onto a random tugboat. You might wonder whether it would be better to seek shelter on land instead. But the unprecedented chaos in Lower Manhattan removed that uncertainty; you had no idea when the next fireball or nuke might come rolling down Wall Street, so you didn't think too hard, just jumped on the boat.

Chapter Twenty-Two

Hobbes's Leviathan Meets the Twin Towers

By now, I hope you're reasonably well assured that a system will develop if your school faces a crisis. But the more thoroughly we understand the causes, the better we can help them develop—and stay out of their way. The lessons of 9/11 are not about mere mechanics but about psychology.

The captains and their boats and communications devices received the lion's share of attention from researchers, movies, and books—but what was going on with the half-million people who went to Battery Park? Their story hasn't been told; it's glossed over with, "Well, going to the park was the obvious thing to do." Not so fast, cub reporter from Channel 6!

Dr. Paul Rapp said recently that to really understand the harbor rescue, you need to understand the rescuees.

As we have learned, psychology and group dynamics are inseparable because individual minds are the moving parts of groups, and the dynamics of groups create systems. Sometimes these systems are long-lasting governments, and sometimes they are a rescue system that lasts for a day.

But some of the ideas behind this research are hundreds of years old, and they are the product of one of the all-time great minds (and instincts) in political philosophy. To really understand the rescue, we need to go to those roots. We're going to talk about Hobbes's *Leviathan* (Hobbes, 1969).

Hobbes based his work on the traditional methods of the time, the foremost being a keen observation of human nature. If you are more comfortable using data-based modern research practices as tools for understanding sociological phenomena, that's understandable. But if you're willing to root around the issue from another angle, new understanding can spring from taking a look at things through a more primitive—but poetic—methodology.

It *is* rather old. In fact, it's so old its author didn't call it a "framework" or a "tool" or a "lens" or a "methodology" at all; he called it a *philosophy*. But although modern researchers have more sciencey-sounding ideas for how we should look at the world, Hobbes had the same motivation: he was trying to erect a scaffolding of reason for figuring out why things happened.

Particularly, he wanted to find the causes behind horrible things. Like those of us who remember the world before 9/11, Hobbes had a lot on his mind. He wanted answers about why the world kept going to hell in a hand-basket. Even if he couldn't stop it, he wanted to understand. If Hobbes had been around on September 11, 2001, he might have argued that a primal survival catalyst was at play during the harbor rescue, and therefore the rescuees were compelled to surrender to the developing rescue force in the interest of self-preservation. Surrender? Yes. They didn't try to overpower the captains and take off with the boats, did they? No, but that wasn't because they weren't afraid.

Hobbes was born in 1588, the year his native England finally defeated the Spanish Armada. A pastor's son, he went to Oxford at fourteen and became a tutor to an aristocratic family. He was an avid scholar but not a voracious reader; a contemporary wrote of Hobbes that he read a fair amount, but what set him apart was his habit of instead spending a great deal of time thinking about what he had read instead of shoveling more undigested material into his mind. As a writer, he was a late bloomer; more charitably, he knew when he was ready to ripen. He didn't write anything until 1629, and it was a translation of Thucydides at that. He seemed fairly content to rehash the classics and enjoy his comfy post with a wealthy family.

But then the devastating English Civil War hit—and this was the catastrophe that inspired the writings that would become *Leviathan.* Hobbes fled England for France to escape the worst of it as he watched his countrymen eat each other alive in a struggle for power. English society shattered from a state of reasonably well-governed order into savage chaos. Hobbes was thunderstruck by the catastrophe. But he had as slow and as careful of a mind as ever; he had to let the horrors of war marinate for a while before he produced his masterwork. Although he published a sort of draft version of his magnum opus in 1642 (the treatise *De Cive*), *Leviathan* wasn't published until he was sixty-three.

He's been called something of a nicer version of Machiavelli, describing the machinations of power with detachment rather than salivating over them. Like Machiavelli, Hobbes saw the struggle between life and death, and between chaos and order, to be fundamental to politics. Sound familiar? The dose of utter chaos that was civil war tore Hobbes out of his bagel and tempered the way he saw things into a full philosophy. His writing didn't glorify war or power-seeking but explained it as he saw it, with a poetic resignation, as a necessary evil: he wrote about what people did to survive in politics.

At first blush, when Hobbes writes about the "Naturall Condition of Mankind," he sounds like a very nice, egalitarian fellow. He writes, "Nature hath made men so equall, in the faculties of body, and mind; as that though there bee found one man sometimes manifestly stronger in body, or of quicker mind then another; yet when all is reckoned together, the difference between man, and man, is not so considerable, as that one man can thereupon claim to himselfe any benefit, to which another may not pretend, as well as he." In other words, all people are more or less the same model, with minor variations, so pretending that you should get to eat all the pie and your neighbor deserves none makes no sense. Awww, sweet.

So far, so good. But the very next sentence gets a little more sinister: "For as to the strength of body, the weakest has strength enough to kill the strongest, either by secret machination, or by confederacy with others, that are in the same danger with himselfe."

Uh . . . yeah. So the upshot of human equality is that because nobody really *deserves* all the pie, but we each kind of *want* all the pie, then we're pretty much always going to be conniving to stab each other in the back over it. And the guy or gal who looks like they're maybe getting an extra blueberry is the first we're going to cut up. That is, unless we figure out a way to organize ourselves to keep the knives sheathed.

To Hobbes, people are plagued by these two forces: the desire for power and everyone *else's* annoying desire for power. Everyone would be all for power struggles if they could just concentrate on conniving, but watching your back is a pain in the neck (it would be centuries before Sartre sputtered that "hell is other people," but surely this is a precursor).

A few people enjoy constant drama, but most would rather be left alone if they can't have all the pie.

Therefore, power tends to coalesce into a formal government because most people can't be bothered to micromanage their power relationships to everyone and everything around them—they would rather outsource that headache, thank you very much.

In other words, people are built to look for a legitimate authority and then accept the common rule of that authority. We seek a font of power to explain things and order things, from our impulse toward religion to our impulse to hand over our total freedom in favor of a legitimate authority. It is when the rules have broken down—like in the English Civil War—that a genius like Hobbes can peer in and see the way the gears work when it comes to deciding what constitutes a legitimate authority.

Hobbes is the guy who famously declared the natural condition of man's life to be nasty, brutish, and short. In a "state of nature"—his term for war, near-war, and general chaos—there are no hippies singing Joan Baez. There are small powers struggling with other small powers to become the big dog. Order isn't natural—chaos is. We have to create order; fortunately, we crave it. Who wants brutish and short?

So people naturally wish to defer to what Hobbes called "the sovereign." This doesn't mean a king. In fact, it is not a person but an office or a structure, an "artificial man." There is a space for authority to fill at the center of our psychological conception of how an ordered society should run, and we are always looking for a person or authority to fill that space. (Jargon like "psychological conception" didn't exist in Hobbes's time, but philosophers like him provided the base concepts that made it possible.)

This is because without this sovereign, overarching power, the power struggles between individuals will result in a gradual upward coalition of power anyway. This end result of the agglomeration of power is what he calls "the Leviathan," named after a giant sea monster from the Bible that ate everything in its path. (Unlike Machiavelli, Hobbes was resigned to the accumulation of power but also awed and slightly dismayed.)

For example, if the U.S. government didn't exist, Hobbes might argue, individual corporations would continue swallowing each other up until the largest, most powerful corporation emerged—Giant Sea Predator, Inc.—thereby creating a power so large that it would effectively function as a government anyway.

This is what people instinctively sense when they cry "Democrats and Republicans are all the same anyway!"—it's one Leviathan or the other. Small powers will always coalesce into a Leviathan, so we might as well try to have a small, orderly, minimally horrid government so we can tame that monster as best we can.

And in a state of chaos, when local ties to the Leviathan have been severed, either a brutish warlord will emerge out of power struggles . . . or people will happily gravitate to a legitimate source of authority. The latter happens when people have agreed to what Hobbes calls "the social contract."

The social contract is a general agreement that instead of warring all against all in a quest to overpower our neighbors and take their stuff—instead of everyone trying to become a successful warlord—we will organize society based on an orderly structure, and we will all follow the rules.

As we are all nearly equal, most of us are willing to give up the slim and pretty much random chance we would have to become the warlord in order to eliminate warlords and replace them with "the sovereign." This is why the rescuees surrendered to the boat captains. The core of the social contract is this: we've agreed to create a tame beast together in hopes that it can keep that really awful sea monster at bay.

In an emergency, following the social contract means not looting stores, not violating passers-by, and not grabbing the rescue boat and paddling off for Yonkers all by yourself, but gravitating to legit authority in an orderly fashion. And on 9/11, as local systems broke down under the chaos, the social contract still held.

This was in part because Admiral Loy quickly emerged as the best person to fill the spot of the sovereign; he was the Leviathan for the day. The chaos shook people around until they converged on a guy who knew what he was doing. Lucky for New York!

And it really was lucky. The social contract sounds nice, but it can be a delicate thing even at the best of times. If things really start to hit the fan—if somebody is going to starve or there are twenty more people than the rescue boats can hold—people can revert to a state of nature with startling speed.

When groups of people are clinging to life, the greatest threat may not be the harsh environment or imminent attack but the other survivors on the harbor front.

Often in dysfunctional survivor groups a division quickly appears between the healthy and strong and the weak and sick. Survivor math's reasoning works like this: if there is a set number of people consuming limited provisions, and it is likely that some will die in a few days anyway, why should the group waste precious food or water on the dying? Sometimes this means abandoning them, but at other times the calculation is much more ruthless.

Warring tribes may have developed and placed fissures in the united front of the social contract as well. Modern researchers, in survival situations, often cite the Robber's Cave experiment (which famously divided a culturally homogenous group of young WASPS into two teams in a semi-survival setting in which they immediately became furiously warring tribes).

Had the rescue lasted more than nine hours, if there were bottlenecks or a shortage of boats, then the rescuee group might have clumped into people who got to the park early versus late arrivers, or into their actual ethnicities or other more permanent categories. At some point, had the lines not kept inching forward, people would have weighed self-preservation, resulting in either "eat the weak" or tribal conflict.

But as with so many things on 9/11, they were lucky. The process was smooth, there were enough boats—and the United States, at least at the time, had a fairly strong social contract.

As people were born into a civil society, they had been indoctrinated to giving up some liberties to the sovereign in order to enjoy security. (And through the transference dynamic as well, they were able to extend that tolerance for the sovereign to the harbor fleet.) This is why we tolerate passports: it means convicted murderers who want to flee one country for another need a passport too.

After 9/11, we took our tolerance for this tradeoff of liberty to a bit of an extreme. Our Congress passed the Patriot Act, which gave the huge and permanent sovereign we call the U.S. government the power to monitor our communications and bank transactions, make us take our socks off at airports, pay for ICE, etc.—all for the trade of security—and most of us willingly complied. Not because we enjoy getting felt up by rent-a-cops at LaGuardia but because humans desire some form of state.

You can see this in schools very clearly. Parents are already willing to go along with most "school safety" measures, even the silly ones. That trend will only continue with the exchange of privacy and liberty for perceived safety. (Eventually, we will have nothing left to give to the state, but I guess we'll blow up that bridge when we come to it.)

So safety isn't a hard sell at all, it's just that what's being sold is all surface-level, direct-cause stuff. It's like walking through the outdoors section of a retailer and buying the nifty tent, shiny thermos, and nubby boots—and then heading into the wild to become disoriented, panic, and end up as a coyote turd.

On 9/11, the state was under attack and potentially crumbling. Remember, there were also planes headed for the Pentagon and the White House, and it was totally plausible that the worst might be yet to come, up to and including a nuke or nukes.

So humans in Lower Manhattan were suddenly—for the first time, for most of them—without their artificial man (the state) and teetering on the brink of a return to their common condition. They were staring into the maw of the war of all against all—kind of the Robber's Cave experiment-type stuff but to-the-death survival.

A reminder of the precious social contract presented itself in the form of the boat rescue force, in other words; it became the artificial man and that, along with the ingredients of transference and pareidolia, served to justify to the rescuees the need to stand in line and get onto the boats in an orderly fashion. It was an easy sell, perhaps, as the alternative was to fight for the boats against a mass of near equals. Cooperation increased your chances, as long as everybody else stayed the course. Because nobody became the first to break the social contract, it held fast.

Hours later, however, when the people were rescued and it was apparent that the government was still intact, the social construct of the harbor dissipated and the previous social contract with the authentic government (which was familiar—a known torus) was accepted as the replacement.

This also is a natural tendency to return to normalcy, or the familiar bagel. So the rescuees might have substituted life buoys for bagels for a few hours. It worked, as they had all lost their appetites.

However, there are dangers inherent in the social contract; for example, it is not always obvious when someone intends to breach it.

For example, here's a mind-bending thought experiment: imagine a similar 9/11 attack in NYC in the year 2041. Instead of human captains negotiating boats into a rescue force, it's all automated through AI, autonomous craft, and overhead drones directing people where to go.

The boat captains and crews did a hell of a job, but what they did was laminated to a moment in time. That type of human-based rescue force after a singularity probably won't happen again—ever. But the psychological factors that we've noted—the torus, transference, pareidolia, Hobbes's Leviathan and the social contract—would all still be very much unchanged in the future.

But the social contract has changed for today's kids (tomorrow's parents/ adults); their social contract is with the phone—that's their tribe. So we have to adjust our rescue force to interact with that form of tribe or else the people will never go to the harbor, even though the robots and craft will await them.

Here's the twist: What if hackers simulate the "tribe" via smartphone tech? We know that puppeteered avatars hooked a million loyal followers on social media. Duped fans were fixated on posts from whom they believed was a living, breathing person, and computer-generated characters become more "life-like" as realistic graphics are coupled to refined algorithms.

Unless we teach kids to verify the sources of their information—most of the commoners already do a really horrible job of this—we might watch thousands of civilians offer themselves up into a hostage situation. Remember Orson Welles? His *War of the Worlds* radio broadcast was another example of people believing what they hear, even if it doesn't have face validity. A generation that instinctively trusts electronic messages is vulnerable. So how might we begin to think about teaching kids to check their sources during a crisis? Imagine the nightmare of a hacked popular avatar unfurling a campaign of harm to self or harm to others.

This is one of the new undersea obstacles we face in guiding today's Leviathan. ("What's this safety manual about?" "Bagels and whales.") In some ways tech has ensured that our kids are safer than ever, but those are also the avenues where they are open to unprecedented vulnerabilities.

The 9/11 generation didn't have to worry about being scammed during a rescue by a virtual sea captain. And let's not forget the effects of those shrunken bagels—the limited experience today's students have with handling mild dangers, such as walking to the park. As savvy as they are to tech and even scams, because they are so unused to venturing outside their narrow pathways, they may not have the presence of mind during a crisis to wonder if the messages they get are legit.

They'll be freaking out, grasping at anything. They are perfectly primed to panic, trust blindly to their phones, and walk into a trap. It sounds far-fetched, but so did 9/11. The actual crisis will no doubt be different from what I'm predicting; in fact, it will probably be more bizarre still.

Therefore, we have to work very hard as educators and parents to at least protect that one-mile roaming radius we still allow our kids. It's not 50 or

130 miles, but it's something, and once it's gone, it's gone. As brilliant as he was, the thing that Hobbes doesn't seem to give sufficient warning against is the fact that it is almost impossible to recover liberties once we surrender them—not without a breakdown and reboot of the social contract. Who wants that?

September 11 was the catalyst for a stronger social contract with the state, and for the most part, we handed over liberties without much or any real debate as we had experienced the horror of the attacks and were very open to trading liberties for security. And it seems that we continue down this path as there is a palpable movement toward socialism and the Patriot Act was reauthorized and expanded without resistance. Futurists talk about school safety being RFID bracelets or implants—it seems we might already be on that path—and would there even be substantial resistance if parents felt that their children would be "safe" at school?

September 11 was awful—and nothing close to it has happened since. Why? From the perspective of the terrorists, they met their objectives. So we'll never know this as it's classified, but likely the intelligence community's threat detection systems have been markedly improved since 9/11. Assuming threat detection has prevented another sentinel attack, wouldn't we want to adopt a similar approach with our schools and school shootings?

In the next decade we will observe a move away from students attending school five days a week from 8:00 a.m. to 3:00 p.m. Why? Students will be taking more courses online—from home or from the bagel shop. What will the safety induction process be like for students who are only in the brick-and-mortar school two days per week? There will need to be some massive shifts in how we think about safety as education is all about structure.

The student safety forum of 2030 might consist of four students sitting at a table and four other students participating from home via video conferencing (not to confuse this with homeschooling). We are nowhere close to prepared for the safety and crisis response factors that need to be solved for the hybrid of online with brick-and-mortar service delivery model that is barreling down on us. So yeah, the book can close with a stark message that by focusing so much on today's "perceived" threats, we've not taken one look to the horizon, and we are investing in theoretical battleships that are already obsolete.

Part V

How We Know What We Know

SO WHY DO THESE SYSTEMS DEVELOP?

Introduction: So, systems will develop. Never fear, just learn to get out of their way. In this lesson, you will learn more about the mechanisms behind why this is so.

Some of them are related to the ideas from Hobbes that we've just discussed—more of that in a moment. Others can be summed up by biological instincts and generic tacit learning; for example, people seem to come pre-programmed to learn to walk and learn their first language. A lot of learning doesn't require being the recipient of explicit teaching, including a lot of social behavior—as well as survival behavior.

This is another reason why our hysterically linear current methods of safety education are so badly misguided; much of what safety education should ideally consist of is *unlearning* bad habits and social cues that cause us to override our best survival instincts. "Get out of their way" is a good rule of thumb when it comes to personal best instincts as well as for systems.

Chapter Twenty-Three

Simulated Annealing

How the Human Brain Is Specialized for Improvisation

If you're sharp, the last chapter of lesson 4 may have left you scratching your head. Okay, you're thinking. So the system converged on Admiral Loy because he was the best guy for the job that day, and all the players on the board shook down until they were headed in his direction and then followed his authority.

But most of those paper pushers in Manhattan had no idea the guy even existed. They might not have even known who he was *after* the rescue, in fact. So how did all those rescuees *know* that the guy they should listen to was some random sea dude? Or even where he was? How did the system shake down in his direction?

In the opinion of one of the top chaos theory experts around (it's great work if you can get it), the answer is: they didn't need to know where they were headed. According to the aforementioned Dr. Paul Rapp, the rescuees just needed to know that they wanted to head in the best possible direction. Once people have agreed tacitly to the social contract, even during a disaster, they have agreed to start scanning for the best answers.

Yeah? So?, you're still thinking. Fortunately, there is yet another oddity in the human mind's operating system that automates this process. It feeds into disaster situations such as 9/11: it's called simulated annealing. Like the torus, simulated annealing is part of chaos theory; it is a concept you need to help dig past the Leviathan, to burrow even further into the roots of disaster psychology.

So . . . simulated what? Annealing is a term swiped from metalworking. In metallurgy, annealing is a heat injection process that is used to improve and purify metals or glass. You add heat to the system—your metal—and let it cool slowly, so the atoms in the material can rearrange themselves into a structure that is better suited to your project; you choose your methods of heating and cooling based on whether you want your material to be harder or more flexible.

This is *sort of* a decent metaphor for simulated annealing. Simulated annealing in chaos theory uses computer simulations to shake down data and algorithms to try to get to the answer that is best suited to your purposes, injecting "heat" in the form of chaos.

Researchers use simulated annealing when they're faced with a problem that can have many solutions, some better than others, but none of them obviously the best. Using a computer simulation, you run many algorithms to find the best one. However, simply running algorithms can result in getting stuck on a "local optimum"—that is, the best answer within a certain area of problem solving—when there may be better answers. So researchers will inject noise into the system to shake things up so they don't get stuck on the nearest optimum.

Dr. Rapp explains this using a common analogy: imagine a lost hiker in the mountains. Mountains don't usually look like a simple cone; they are jagged with many peaks that go up and down. Our hiker is down in a valley among the mountain peaks, with no idea where a familiar landmark is, or even whether he is near the top of the mountain he is on.

Most educated people, if lost this way, will either sit tight and wait for rescuers to find them or will try to get to a high peak for a better view of the area. If our hiker sees a few peaks before him, he will climb to the top of what looks like the highest peak in his vicinity to see what things look like from there.

If, once atop that peak, he sees that he is nowhere near the highest point on the mountain—that now all he sees are other even higher peaks around him—he will sigh, climb back down that peak, and head in the direction of what, from the peak he was on, looks like the highest vantage point. Eventually, he hopes to get to a place from which he can see past these noisy peaks to some landmark that will tell him where he is. However, if he is running out of calories and night is falling, at some point he will just have to go with the least bad possible route he has seen so far and hope for the best.

Rapp proposes that your brain does a similar thing in a crisis. The rescuees' individual acts of simulated annealing helped turn the potential chaos of the Lower Manhattan rescue into an orderly procedure.

When your mind takes in the available facts of a situation—what you can see from the crag where you've begun—and uses simulated annealing on them, it looks at the data around you and quickly runs algorithms to move from solution to solution, trying to move from a less optimal state to a more optimal state.

Once you've reached that first not-so-bad state, you size the situation back up and run the program again from there, trying to arrive at the most optimal solution that you can get to in the limited amount of time you have to decide. To put it more simply, in simulated annealing, a person moves through solutions, switching from less to more optimal states to try to find the most optimal solution he or she can in the time that he or she has.

Simulated annealing in the organization of cognitive processes is an idea that has been discussed in the safety community for several years. However, there is very little that has found its way into print, and by most accounts the development of the simulated annealing framework is a work in progress.

CLIMBING THE MOUNTAIN

To engage in simulated annealing means that one is open to reconnaissance and appropriate functioning within a state of chaos. What we assume in simulated annealing is that people always accept a candidate decision if it is better that the incumbent (their tentative choice) and that they usually reject a candidate if it is equal to or worse than the incumbent. Simulated annealing has no way of determining whether a given decision is globally optimal or not. There's too much stuff in the world. But it is a good model to avoid being stuck on a local optimum.

If you're stuck in one crag on the mountaintop, for example, you may not even be aware that there is a deep valley below housing a village full of potential rescuers. Once you reach the summit, the village below reveals itself and you are no longer a lost person. But had that deep valley been barren, you would have expended resources and further distanced yourself from searchers. Simulated annealing is probability—it's weighing risk and reward—and was part of hundreds of thousands of rescues on 9/11.

You must exercise simulated annealing in order to not lock yourself into small depressions along the slope of the mountain; in other words, you continue to respond when noise is injected into the system.

When you find yourself in a noisy, chaotic environment, the best thing to do is to allow that chaos to foster creative thought and flexibility of behavior. In fact, you should inject a bit more chaos yourself if need be. If you're sitting on your butt on a mountain crag wondering what to do while your calorie stores burn out, you need to do something, get up, climb to a higher peak, or go back down; by refusing to add more chaos you're pretty much doomed to croak.

But too often we are trained to lock on to conventional behaviors in a crisis situation. Yes, it's necessary to build basic muscle and spatial memory, such as knowing where the exits are. But if you can't get to a particular exit, and you can't do anything else you've planned to do, you need to know how and when to kick over the board. This is nonlinear thinking—you are engaging in the domain of nonlinear dynamics.

Another common analogy to describe how systems (or people) can get trapped in local minima is imagining a ball bearing rolling on a puzzle board with multiple levels of depressions. If simulated annealing in the form of an immense amount of noise is added to the system, it shakes the ball bearings loose from the local minimum and gets them to flow toward the global minimum—that is, toward the "creative state."

On 9/11, Rapp says, the puzzle board was shaken so hard the balls could not avoid the creative state: "The chaos was liberating from the conventionalities of behavior." And the tragedy was so vast that it had a numbing effect; things that might have paralyzed people with fear under ordinary circumstances were met with a shocked nod: sure, okay.

How did simulated annealing look during the 9/11 boat rescue? Everyone in Lower Manhattan was eager to leave local safe-seeming optima—hiding under a sturdy structure or diving down a manhole—to move toward a better solution, culminating in escaping the island. One reason to embrace chaos was motivation—you were motivated by self-preservation (*my manhole might flood or catch on fire anyway*), comfort (*maybe I can get home to Yonkers and drink a six-pack or three?*), or to reestablish tribal unification (*where are my family and friends?*).

The boats in New York Harbor didn't just show up and ferry individual passengers wherever they wanted to go as though they were Ubers; that would have created total chaos. Instead, as they walked toward New York Harbor, the rescuees could see the boat captains raising makeshift signs, such as white bedsheets, with destination locations spray painted on them, such as "Hoboken."

While Hoboken might not be the optimal destination if you're trying to leave the island and get home to Yonkers, it represents a step closer to a target destination. Hence, by getting on the boat to Hoboken, you would be leaving a lesser suboptimal option for a better but still suboptimal option, which would be Hoboken.

Once at Hoboken, you would have a new set of destination options to mull over. It might take several transfers, with completely new options to select from, until one arrives at one's desired location or optimized outcome.

After the boat to Hoboken, the person might need to take a bus, car, train, or walk—whatever—to finally get home. Another example: your plane trip from London to Chicago is canceled. However, you can fly to Detroit and then catch a bus to Chicago, so hey, new plan. That's simulated annealing: trading suboptimal outcomes for what you believe will be better outcomes. This isn't foolproof, and it is a bit scary. So my sense is that today's youth would settle on a suboptimal outcome.

Chaos theorists consider annealing to be effective at finding good decisions for difficult optimization problems, but it requires a substantial amount of computational effort. It turns out that one often gets the best result by starting out with relatively frequent irrational jumps and then slowly reducing the frequency of irrational jumps in favor of rational descent.

Start from chaos alternating with reason, then slowly reduce chaos and increase reason, and that leads you to a better result than reason alone.

On 9/11, therefore, the varying waves of chaos had different effects on people's behavior. The extreme chaos of the explosions first pushed the rescuees away from the falling buildings because the danger was obvious—they had only one choice.

Then the continued but less acute chaos, through a mental process similar to simulated annealing—and also through the group dynamics of following each other—herded them toward Battery Park, largely because they had nowhere else to go and perhaps because their past experience had already suggested to them that government systems might provide some kind of rescue if they could get to the shore.

Most of the ball bearings shook down to the lowest (most optimal) spot on the game board, to use the ball-bearing analogy. Once there, the chaos was such that, even if the captains were not the Navy and the boats were listing, nobody had many second thoughts about climbing aboard, even if the boat was headed for Hoboken and they lived in Yonkers; they could shake their way down from there. In the end, among all of the chaotic events, an incredible half-million people were brought to safety in a more or less orderly fashion.

Chapter Twenty-Four

Leadership Theories After Hobbes

At the risk of skirting intellectual idol worship, it's hard to look at modern leadership theorists without seeing how much they owe to Hobbes's work (whether they know it, like it, or not). Particularly in instances in which systems break down, Hobbes's instincts for observing the gravitation toward leadership and hierarchies that humans can't seem to avoid were sublime.

One example comes from evolutionary leadership theory. These theorists, unlike Hobbes, also have biological evolution as a concept to draw from. However, a strict "survival of the fittest" interpretation of Darwin makes the rescuees' behavior actually look kind of confusing. How would a species evolve members who don't just elbow each other out of the way? If you were in Battery Park on 9/11 and you waited patiently in line for a boat instead of grabbing the boat for yourself, your behavior seems optimized to ensure the greatest possible percentage of the group escapes . . . but not necessarily *you.*

As evolutionary leadership theorist Dawkins put it (1976), "it is not obvious why people agree to subordinate themselves when this may put them at an evolutionary disadvantage (Van Vugt, Hogan, & Kaiser, 2008, p. 189)" as far as getting mates and other prestige-related prizes go (such as not drowning in New York Harbor or getting killed by a possible nuke). And yet they do.

According to evolutionary leadership theorists, the answer lies in looking at a population as a kind of organism in itself—one that needs to adapt or die, just like the design of an individual animal.

Some theorists suggest that followership emerged in response to specific ancestral problems that were best solved through collective effort coordinated by a leader-follower structure that enhanced individual and group survival. It was just more efficient to have one guy at the head of things. This implies that leader–follower patterns will emerge more quickly and effectively in circumstances that mirror the kind of problems that take us back to our primordial roots (for example, internal group conflict, immediate external threats).

So, if "survival of the fittest" and leadership behavior seem to be at odds, it's because you aren't considering the population as what it is: a larger creature that needs to evolve, just like individuals' genetics do. Where Hobbes saw the body politic, modern theorists are beginning to see what is called a "superorganism" (Bloom, 1997).

This is another interesting contribution from Howard Bloom, who, when he's not using bagels to describe physics or doing publicity for little musical acts like Michael Jackson (true story), he also adds Darwin to Hobbes in a way that furthers Dawkins's ideas about leadership and evolution. Bloom sees a population as a larger biological unit, not just a larger political unit.

What Hobbes sees as the sovereign is, in Bloom's view, less about the sheer mechanics of a political system and more akin to a biological metaphor. The body politic is a large creature made of smaller creatures, the way your cells contain tiny structures that, eons ago, used to be separate species and were symbiotically engulfed by larger ones. The sovereign translates to the "brain" of a larger creature made up of the individuals; like the cells in your toe are part of you, you are a cell in the superorganism, and the governing bodies are the nervous system.

So if you built Bloom's idea onto Dawkins, you realize that leadership and followership are a function of being a cell in a "creature" that has survived because these behaviors worked for it in the past.

Therefore, it made sense for the rescuees in the park to cooperate rather than grab the boats, in the way that it makes sense for your toe to follow along as you walk rather than grabbing the foot and going off to scavenge for glucose on its own.

Or if you prefer to look at it through Hobbes's logic, that works too: it *did* make sense on a selfish, rational level for the thinking man or woman, who realizes that because all people are nearly equal you probably can't overpower all the other individuals and grab the boat. We follow leadership (but sometimes disobey) because we are social creatures with some individual drives. The individual survival instinct and the group instincts need to balance each other out, and evolution has worked pretty hard on us to make sure that they do.

To put it in more familiar terms: it might have occurred to you to grab the boat, but it would seem more natural to most people to cooperate, for reasons most of us probably can't explain.

They're probably a mix of nature and nurture; yes, you've always been taught to cooperate, but there's an evolutionary reason why you are wired to learn cooperation and not to revert automatically to selfish behavior in an emergency. (At least not until the excrement really hits the air circulation device.)

Dawkins's earlier theory does not go quite as far as Bloom's (that's how ideas in linear time generally progress), but it is more widely accepted by the academic community; nonetheless, even Dawkins's hypothesis has not been tested explicitly.

However, it is consistent with prior findings. People are more likely to follow under conditions of threat—for example, during natural disasters or intergroup conflicts (Baumeister et al., 1988). Van Vugt and De Cremer (1999) showed that leaderless groups negotiate internal conflicts less effectively in times of crisis. And again in the famous Robber's Cave experiment, when faced with team competition, the two groups of schoolboys promptly chose team leaders (Sherif et al., 1961).

Followers also prefer different leaders depending on the problem they face. U.S. voters tend to choose hawkish presidents when threatened by war (McCann, 1992) and to show an increased preference for charismatic leaders and a decreased preference for participative leaders when reminded of their mortality (Cohen et al., 2004). There isn't much mention in the accounts of the 9/11 rescue of Admiral Loy's capacity for charm; *Boatlift* was narrated by Tom Hanks, who did most of the talking, and Loy only showed up in a few clips. He wasn't even on the scene during the rescue, in fact; according to Dr. Paul Rapp, Loy was at the Coast Guard headquarters in Washington, DC, during the crisis.

However, one of the key things to keep in mind about transference and legitimate authority is that they in fact must not be confused with charm. History is full of examples of entire populations mistaking charm for legit authority, the obvious go-to being Adolf Hitler, but the 9/11 rescuees and ship captains did not commit that error.

To this day Loy has never capitalized on 9/11 to market himself; he could have made millions just presenting about what he did on 9/11, doing movies and motivational speaking and college commencements—and he didn't. He just got half a million people to safety and slow faded off the stage.

Chapter Twenty-Five

Legacy Knowledge, Distributed Leadership, and Rookie Teachers vs. Admiral Loy

Finally, a word on the practical reasons behind the need for legacy knowledge and distributed leadership.

There's nothing wrong with the Internet.

But there are extremely practical underpinnings to the desire to preserve some kind of continuity—dear God, any kind of continuity—of knowledge among the staff in our schools. No, Google is *not* an adequate substitute for being shown the ropes. The problem with being ignorant, after all, is not knowing what you don't know. (If you Google "stuff I don't know that I need to know," you get a listicle on how to figure out whether your bellybutton is normal.) The preservation of knowledge about a facility and the way it runs comes in handy in ways we never expect. Unfortunately, the way it makes its absence felt are just as surprising—but also unpleasant.

Legacy knowledge increases every actor's options in a crisis. Lack of it means that if your only option takes you in a direction where none of your staff have familiarity, they're up a creek.

Take a new teacher. He's so new that he hasn't yet explored the wing of the building where he doesn't work, for instance. What happens if there is a fire and the only direction that is open to him and his students is toward that unknown string of classrooms? Sure, there have always been one or two teachers on high school campuses who are fresh out of college or otherwise new.

But what if this describes half your staff? What if the reason that new teacher hasn't explored campus is because none of the other teachers have been around long enough for any of them to give him a tour? Don't you wish you had a seasoned teacher around who could have given him an engaging campus tour upon hire?

Well, it's too late. You now have fifty students wandering around a totally unknown floorplan in an inferno. And the teacher in the classroom next door is almost as new as he is, so instead of being able to help him, she's just as confused. So now you have a hundred students running toward the unknown. Hopefully, some of the students know where they're going.

Oh, wait, most of them transferred a semester or two ago. They have a short recess right before this period, but they're so used to being told to avoid the unknown that instead of exploring the campus, they've been sitting at their desks with their smartphones while they wait for the teacher to arrive. Students with narrow toruses plus high staff turnover . . . are you starting to see how dangerous all of these conditions together can become?

Legacy knowledge is also key to another leadership theory idea: distributed leadership. What distributed leadership means is that when there is enough general knowledge in the group, the leader can afford to confidently delegate. She can give those she commands discretion and know that their discretion will be informed.

We've already discussed how discretion is essential in an emergency; well, leaders who don't trust that their followers know enough to use it are not going to be emphatic when giving their followers permission to use discretion.

Go back to the new teacher in the fire. Imagine you're that school's safety officer. You told everybody to use their discretion . . . well, now they're using it at random, all over the burning building. But your only other choice was to give them a flip chart and then watch them freeze like deer in the headlights when the unexpected occurs. Teachers need permission to use discretion, but they also need the ability to use it wisely, which involves making decisions based on their interpretation of in-the-moment situations and contexts.

Legacy information makes leadership distributable, in other words, which frees leaders up to work on the big picture. Compare today's high school principal—just got hired last month, is still burned out from her last two-year gig, barely knows where the cafeteria is—and her team of equally unseasoned teachers to Admiral Loy and his "ragtag" crew of boat pilots, many of whom had been working the area for decades and knew each other and the harbor well.

The tugboat community in New York Harbor considered its members to be something of a family. McAllister Towing, for example, had been serving the harbor since 1864; they put the first diesel tug in New York Harbor, and they were there on 9/11, rescuing people from Battery Park (McAllister Towing and Transportation Co., Inc., 2018). There was knowledge in that organization that could facilitate the rescue in ways even federal troops might not have equaled.

Tugboats comprised the majority of watercraft participating in the harbor rescue, and the tug captains were not just familiar with the area, they were familiar with chaos. As we discussed earlier, leaving your bagel often enough can bring larger and larger portions of the chaos area that lie outside of your torus into what your nervous system will accept as somewhat normal; in other words, people who are accustomed to chaos develop a sort of four- or five-dimensional torus. And then when your choices narrow down due to the limitations of extreme chaos, you recognize that fact right away and act with decision.

Lewis Burwell Puller was a U.S. Marine from the World War II era who has long served as a classic example of leadership in chaos. Better known as "Chesty" Puller, he won five Navy Crosses, one of them for an improvised action that helped him save three American companies from annihilation in the Pacific theater, a kind of miniature one-man Dunkirk; shortly later he led two American infantry units in defending a crucial airfield from enemy attack. Chesty Puller has served as the classic American example of someone who was comfortable with chaos and skilled at helping the soldiers around him embrace it as well (Davis, 2016).

Puller summed up the simplicity of a total chaos situation with his famous line from the Korean War: "We're surrounded. That simplifies the problem" (Davis, 2016; Rapp, personal interview, 2017). Chesty Puller knew the area outside of his bagel like the back of his hand. When you know the outside of the bagel, you are familiar with the harbor from a lifetime on a boat, and total chaos arrives, it almost feels like familiar territory.

Thus, the boat captains were able to convey confidence to the 9/11 rescuees. The rescuees in turn were able to depend on the knowledge base and core competence of boat drivers; the transference dynamic linked to the trust in American institutions that they had been able to develop throughout their lives matched up with the competent improvisation they were seeing unfold. When the captains improvised gangplanks, the rescuees trusted them. Stand in line, wait your turn, get on board, and get out of Manhattan. Would your students have the same level of trust in your staff?

You can also compare teachers' fear of punishment should they make controversial decisions in a crisis to the certainty the boat captains felt on 9/11 that they were free to use their discretion. Once Loy had established the vertical leadership structure of the rescue, he freed his rescuers in no uncertain terms from the burdens of standard operating protocols or the need to make a big bureaucratic deal out of every action before they took it.

Loy instead empowered captains with discretion. *Black's Law Dictionary* defines discretion as "wise conduct and management; cautious discernment; prudence" and "individual judgment; the power of free decision making"

(Garner, 2009). Discretion goes hand in hand with improvisation and calls on experience, tacit knowledge, and the sensemaking skills that are necessary to "read" and "react" to an ever-changing context and situation.

Discretion, by the way, is also something many teachers seem to feel they are not allowed to exercise, resulting in their demands for flip charts and their shyness around improvisation. Perhaps they have become accustomed—via long years of strict government initiatives around the curriculum and other procedural matters—to continually being told exactly what to do. They, too, need to feel more comfortable outside of their torus—a large part of which is simply conferring orders to students from on high rather than exercising true authority in the classroom. In a disaster, these habits could be, well, disastrous.

Stephen Casner, a research psychologist with the National Aeronautics and Space Administration, has been involved in twenty years of civilian and military research examining pilot responses to dynamic situations. The following study underscores how even highly trained individuals experience confusion when presented with abnormal events.

Casner, Geven, and Williams (2013) exposed fatal limitations to standard operating procedures in their study "The Effectiveness of Airline Pilot Training for Abnormal Events." Despite rigorously practiced responses to expected abnormal events, pilots were not diligently trained in problem solving for unscripted and less predictable exercises.

> Numerous accident reports describe situations in which pilots responded to abnormal events in ways that were different from what they had practiced many times before. One explanation for these missteps is that training and testing for these skills have become a highly predictable routine for pilots who arrive to the training environment well aware of what to expect. Under these circumstances, pilots get plentiful practice in responding to abnormal events but may get little practice in recognizing them and deciding which responses to offer. (p. 477)

The researchers questioned pilots who struggled to recognize unfamiliar situations and learned that they experienced confusion and surprise as they perceived variations from expected conditions. Reflecting upon Weick's sensemaking approach (Weick, Sutcliffe, & Obstfeld, 2005), it appears that the pilots failed to rapidly identify the changing environmental and situational contexts and by the time they did, panic displaced rational thought. They simply could not talk their way to sensible decisions (p. 413). Furthermore, it appeared that pilots had little discretion to deviate from strict protocols.

Why didn't the boat captains experience situational confusion similar to that which dogged the pilots in this study?

SEASONED CAPTAINS AND CREWS DEMONSTRATING DISTRIBUTED SENSEMAKING AND DISTRIBUTED LEADERSHIP

Part of the answer involves an idea that is very closely related to discretion: distributed leadership. Up until the past decade or two, we could reliably count on the inculcation of legacy knowledge to staff and students due to the predictable, paced turnover of staff and students. Today, school leaders maintain their posts for a scant span; teachers leave and enter the profession in droves, and student cohort survival rates spiral downward in a transient society as their parents move them from school district to school district.

We have crossed an unfortunate threshold. The constant churn of principals, teachers, and students has driven the theoretical framework of distributed leadership to extinction in some districts and relegated it to the endangered list in the others.

James Spillane (2005) defines leadership as a practice that unfolds among diverse leaders and followers in specific situations. He suggests that leadership is not only shaped by people interacting with one another but also by certain tools and routines they employ in carrying out their work together (p. 146). Examples of tools of practice include safety flip charts and student assessment rubrics. Instances of routines of practice include daily "walk-throughs," weekly collaboration sessions, and fire drills.

As found in Spillane and Orlina (2005, pp. 158–59), "Leadership refers to activities tied to core work of the organization that are designed by organization members to influence the motivation, knowledge, affect, and practices of other organizational members *or* that are understood by organization."

These tools and routines are core, not peripheral, elements of leadership practice in many school situations. Given that there appear to be few formal tools and routines of practice employed around leadership practices that prepare schools to be safe from low-incidence episodes of violence, the *discretion* that leaders use in this domain emerges as an area of educational leadership research that is especially of note. This in-the-moment discretion demarks an evolution from distributed leadership to sensemaking as the desired approach by which to situate school safety decision making. Wall-hanging flip charts are artifacts of an ancient safety world.

Throughout history, the ability to exercise discretion in the best interests of others appears strongest in situations in which the person making the decision feels that the "greater organization" will vindicate the decision.

It's the "I've got your back" principle: if people feel their organization and higher-ups will support any decisions they make in good faith—even if their simulated annealing and the resulting decision are not perfect—then they make better decisions more easily, with less hesitation.

This was as apparent in the September 11, 2001, rescue as it was in the April 29–30, 1975, military evacuation of South Vietnamese citizens and American personnel from Saigon.

Code named Operation Frequent Wind, the speed of the Saigon evacuation and number of people involved created an unforeseen scenario of ships overwhelmed with people and the helicopters that brought them. Some ships struggled to maintain buoyancy.

Orders were given to push surplus helicopters over the sides of the ships to make room for more people. Some pilots dropped off passengers and then ditched their machines at sea. More than seven thousand people were evacuated in Operation Frequent Wind. Commanders that made decisions to plunge aircraft were *not* reprimanded. In fact, *all* personnel who participated in Operation Frequent Wind were authorized the Vietnam Service Medal, Vietnam Cross of Gallantry, and Humanitarian Service Medal (Perrodin, 2017).

However, as hinted earlier, teachers today tend to feel they will receive no such validation or flexibility, in part because of the intense academic testing that is currently taking precedence over everything—from critical thinking to school safety. All schools receive individual report cards from the states these days, and these report cards contain nothing about safety. So schools have an incentive to go heavy on professional development in areas that appear on the report card. In academics, teachers are graded on achievement of criteria not growth toward criteria, which reinforces the very linear thinking patterns we have trained teachers into and keeps them thinking about how to follow set objectives from above rather than dealing with what is before them. Their raises and contract renewals depend on them being hyper linear.

Add this to the deemphasis on safety training, and of course all they want is a flip chart to cling to. We have made their jobs hinge on checking off boxes rather than teaching or engaging in creative or critical thinking. When they are locked into an objective from above during routine operations, it is difficult for them to imagine that their independent judgment in an emergency will be tolerated.

But in fact, allowing teacher discretion in an emergency is locked into our legal system—and you should make it your business to make teachers aware of this. There is a longstanding legal standard that educators should act "in the best interests" of students, which means teachers have the right to use their discretion to determine what is in the students' best interests. Stefkovich and O'Brien (2004) contend that there was no clear definition of "the best interest of the child." Therefore, teachers and the like must use their discretion to make ethically wise decisions to the best of their ability. The discretion and authority afforded school officials must enhance student rights beyond what is provided for in the U.S. Constitution.

The absence of a uniform definition of "best interest" certainly contributes to the prevailing dearth of inter-rater reliability within the reviewed literature, but the impossibility of pinning down a definition—sometimes it's in their best interests to keep them seated; sometimes it's in their best interests to tell them to run like crazy—is what mandates giving teachers free rein.

Begley and Stefkovich also agree that there is no consistent definition of "best interest" of the child: a content analysis of over sixty law review articles using this term ("best interests of the student") or a variation of it (for example, "best interests of students," "best interests of children") revealed no common theme and no shared use (Begley & Stefkovich, 2007, p. 214). And so "best interest" will always be subjective—distilled from individual experiences, biases, perceptions of situations, and dynamic context.

An expert witness offers opinions calibrated to the legal standard known as the "reasonable degree of probability." In layman's terms, he or she makes a determination if the person acted in a manner that would reasonably be expected from a person with similar training, experiences, and skills presented with a similar context and situation. For example, if a student informed a teacher that she was contemplating harm to herself, it would be expected for that teacher to immediately investigate the threats and pursue a course of action to ensure student safety, which probably entails following a school protocol, contacting a school response team, and perhaps calling 911.

Discretion plays an important part in this as it affords the teacher flexibility, but too much discretion can teeter on negligence. This might be when the teacher chooses not to follow the required threat assessment protocol and simply dismisses the student as an attention-seeking drama queen.

Of course, there has to be a balance; too much discretion and there's no consistency from person to person and also no documentation and no records. But we err more often on the side of giving teachers the impression that they rarely have any choice; then this becomes their habit of mind, and they *want* a flip chart for everything so they can feel safe. As we have been, linear thinking makes them *less* safe from intruders, but it makes them *more* safe, in most instances, from reprimands and threats to their livelihood.

Chapter Twenty-Six

Summary of What We Know

Okay, here's the cheat sheet version of the points this book has been driving home so far. Not only does this serve as a summary, but you could also photocopy it and use it in place of a flip chart, if you still have that last unconvinced teacher on your staff who's really got to have one. Maybe if he or she stares at it long enough, reality will sink in.

More seriously, you can use these points as the backbone of a safety presentation among your staff or fellow staff to help you argue clearly for safety innovation in your school.

There are the basic points:

a. The events of 9/11 activated our basic human tendency to follow (followership).
b. Situational leaders emerged in this situation, so now the followers have a leader or leaders to turn to.
c. The transference dynamic is the mechanism that allowed trust to be transferred, allowing the evacuation of five hundred thousand people without any legal, enforced, required, or dictatorial mandate. People followed the developing systems and leaders voluntarily.
d. Improvisation led to quick thinking and action. No need to follow scripted protocols, stage and wait, or measure the effectiveness of the event to benchmarking. These would have not only hindered the rescue but also eroded the rescue structure that subsequently established a toroidal bubble within the chaos.
e. The rescue was an open system, almost a portal, that was self-created only through extreme chaos, and the open system interacted dynamically with the quickly evolving environment.

f. The weather positively contributed to the rescue operations as well as limited the potent mix of terror, despair, and mindless aggression that happens during darkness, as exemplified by the night creature that prowled in the infamous novel *The Lord of the Flies*.

g. The past is never transparent, even with the most careful research and introspection. We do not have the information required for applied decision analysis, and such microfracturing of inquiry would ultimately lead to a linear training and linear response protocols.

h. There is no sameness, only similarity.

LESSON SIX: THE FUTURE

Introduction: Okay, benchmarking is overrated, but we can still take some educated guesses at where we are headed, both from the attackers' point of view and the safety professionals' point of view, and about where we should be headed. There is a difference between the kind of one-to-one mapping that leads most schools and safety professionals astray and the uses of pattern recognition. To overstate the point against sameness is to negate it: the past is what has taught us that the future is always going to be different from the past.

Expressed on a more down-to-earth level: developments don't spring out of thin air. Change is the only constant, as an ever-rotating cast of pessimistic intellectuals has spent most of history trying to tell us. Chaos theory is now telling us they're right. So the following chapters will provide some educated guesses as to where these forces might best be directed. We will discuss some of the underinformed things schools are beginning to do that they should stop doing before it's too late and the costs are sunk; more optimistically, we'll talk about how our options for analyzing and improving school safety can best be studied and what we can do to improve.

Chapter Twenty-Seven

How Will Decisions Made in the Moment Be Studied? And How Will Future Decisions Be Directed?

School leaders need to be careful not to immobilize teachers with a million rules when it comes to disaster responses. They should also be free of fear; except in cases of malice or gross negligence, teachers should not be disciplined for decisions made in crises, even if they don't work out. If one teacher is punished for a crisis response, the next will remember this and freeze. They should be worried *only* about survival, not about looking good and keeping their job.

But this doesn't mean we can't study crisis reactions, analyze the decision-making process, and try to come up with ways to make teacher discretion (and disaster handling in general) more effective. Although the improvement of cell phone technology has helped safety as a side benefit, we don't have to wait for another advance from outside the safety profession. It's not just advances in technology that influence crisis preparedness and responses. A huge leap forward right now could come from simple introspection: from looking into the way we look at looking into things. Okay, maybe that's not so simple.

Researchers need to examine their own torus—the familiar little bubble of their profession. They surround themselves with the same ideas, the same stilted and sometimes obscurantist academic language, every day.

But under all the fifty-cent words, they have succumbed to a horrible lack of critical thinking and an adhesion to groupthink. Too many researchers accept ideas simply *because they have become part of their torus* when they should be judging them based on evidence. Oh, the public is used to going through metal detectors at airports? Well then, metal detectors will make schools safe, right?

Metal detectors tell people they're in the "safe" part of our bagel, near the doughy center. But academics don't get paid by society to wallow in the middle of the mental bagel. They are supposed to be on the edges, or at least ask questions about how what's in the center got there. Researchers are paid, in this case, to recognize that although a metal detector might signal "safe" in a familiar way, an airport and a high school are laid out in completely different ways.

To get even *more* postmodern, the academic bagel colors researchers' thoughts about everything from familiar theories to new crises—as does the rest of their history. Life experiences and psychological influences shape their biases and ability to identify and assign a pattern to behaviors—just as a victim's past changes his or her behavior in a crisis, researchers analyzing the crisis will change their perspective based on their well of experience and knowledge. However, the tools for studying crisis reactions are so clumsy, particularly when you try to include the interaction of our personal histories, that they shake one's faith in the value of studying past crises at all.

Or even drills. Take After Action Reports (AARs), which sound more exciting than they are, are reports you write after a drill to note how things went. They don't follow a universal template. They try to boil things down in a strictly linear fashion: Was this rescue response action good or was it bad? Well, the field of battle is often wide, and what was optimal in the school gym perhaps didn't work out so well for another group that got caught in the hall.

Further, they don't capture the difference between the way one firefighter, for example, might respond to circumstances in a slightly different way from another, even in the same department with the same training. These tidy documents might tell the tale of the event from the collective qualitative perspective, but what is sorely missing are the personal backstories—the lived experiences that created each responder.

In previous chapters we peered into the psychological and sociological backstory that created the 9/11 rescuees and made their cooperation with the rescue seem natural. So what about the rescuers?

If some of the police staff handled the crisis well, was it because they had more training, or was it that they were afforded more discretion? We don't know, because the AARs just tell us "She handled it well," "He didn't know where the other responding units were," or "He took the lead." Departments try to adjust using this surface information, but we don't fund studies after sentinel events to do deep dives into the backgrounds of individual responders.

It's largely an unknown landscape, and with a little research spending, this is an exciting area for study. What if we could find out that there is a profile of an effective responder for a specific sentinel event?

There isn't much research out there, which is a shame and an opportunity. But tentatively, the studies that do exist suggest there is also some type of transference dynamic at play with the responders.

These folks are largely a dark spot in our knowledge; safety funding is usually flooded into fortification and equipment. But a potential research study could dig into the experiences of individual responders: What size was their hometown? Did they travel? Did they experience major emotional traumas or sentinel disasters themselves during childhood? What courses did they take in college? And so on. There is plenty of software that can reveal correlation, and strength of correlation, among multiple variables.

Such research would be fascinating if you could get funding to do it on professional responders, but it would be even *more* interesting if you could also apply it to Cajun Navy Relief volunteers and then compare the two groups. Cajun Navy Relief was an originally spontaneous but amazingly effective citizen corps; it's unlikely that the efficiency of their response would be correlated to any type of formal ICS or safety/rescue training. (To refine the study, you could eliminate volunteers who did have some formal training or weight for the amount of training.) You could identify the variables in their lives that both contributed to and detracted from their effectiveness in crisis.

The results could be as simple as discovering that older rescuers are more effective in one type of crisis than in another, or they could be groundbreaking, stripping bare the relative value of simple situational awareness compared to specific training or equipment. What if you found that teaching situational awareness correlated significantly with rescue effectiveness—or even more strongly than formal training on rescue techniques? Departments might be looking at a huge leap forward in safety effectiveness without having to spend a dime on equipment. Talk about taking the profession outside of its bagel!

So climbing back down from that lofty hypothetical peak—documents like the AAR are shallow and miss data on responders, as well as missing specific data about the rescuees.

But they also tend to incorrectly benchmark tools to standards present at the time of the event.

When the Twin Towers were built in 1970, they were designed to withstand the impact of a Boeing 707 aircraft, the largest aircraft being flown at that time. The Boeing 767 aircraft used in the September 11 attack were considerably larger. The structural resilience of the towers was perfectly adequate for 1970; against a 2001 aircraft, however, they crumpled into rubble.

We can't know what's coming. And yet, too often, we develop linear plans for what will be nonlinear events. For example, say the groundskeeper at an elementary school backs the lawnmower into the natural gas meter, releasing a giant flammable cloud. The building must be evacuated. The evacuation site is a church two blocks away. The fire department issues a six-block evacuation radius. This doesn't fit any of our drills! Now what? Are staff going to be able to cope with this? It depends on whether we are spending countless hours teaching stereotyped patterns that only work in a narrow band of instances—protecting our schools from one hundred out of any of the millions of patterns of screwiness that could face them—or whether we are teaching situational awareness and sensemaking.

Our intent shouldn't be to dampen variability—to shrink the torus and encase it in titanium. As Dr. Rapp says, "What we know is that a high degree of variability is in fact a good thing and even, say, applying chaos theory to biological analysis." He uses heartbeat patterns as an example: "A reliable indicator of health is heart rate variability. . . . High heart rate variability inter-beat sequence is an indication of health."

In other words, you know your ticker is working well not because you have a normal overall heart rate but because your heart can vary its rate depending on what you're doing that second and then adapt to your next activity.

In pathological conditions, Rapp says, the heart adapts with less flexibility; going with the flow of chaos, on the other hand, is a marker of health. "A chaotic system is one which keeps on searching the behavior space, and it is much more likely to come up with a good effective solution by virtue of that behavior space search." Like your heart scanning for the right time to beat, the rescuees in Battery Park were, in part, searching their behavior space for an effective solution.

In other words, our responses, to be healthy and create a healthy response system, need to be and remain as flexible as possible. However, there's a paradox in that statement: it means that we need to be inflexibly flexible. Which means coming up with a way to reinforce to our entire consciousness that our go-to should be outside the comfort zone. This largely ties into one steady idea: Keep it simple, stupid. Which means that we may not need a flip chart, but we do need a mantra.

Run-hide-fight is the current intruder mantra. Dr. Rapp notes that military doctrine is communicate-move-shoot. That's pretty close; communicating and thinking are related phenomena. But as proposed earlier, in line with relevant research and observations, a better idea is: Embrace, Assess, Inventory, and Decide.

Additional research on safety knowledge acquisition and dissemination within and across schools would promote legislation that is based on empirical evidence and research versus reactionary measures suited to public outcry following a tragic safety event.

But legislators know that their constituency is more interested in action than research; it's like we're all still cowboys, forming a vigilante gang and to heck with the judge and jury. "After the devastating school shootings in Newtown, Connecticut, in December 2012, state lawmakers around the country vowed to act. The mission: devise ways to prevent a similar tragedy," wrote Edweek reporters Shah and Ujifusa in 2014. Empirical research gets trampled as the public rushes legislators following a high-profile school safety incident. The Sandy Hook Elementary School shooting, which was the deadliest school shooting in the United States, pressured legislators to provide a rapid response to appease a very nervous constituency.

Shah and Ujifusa (2014) reveal that "an analysis of more than 450 bills related to school safety filed within 6 months after the deadliest K–12 school shooting in U.S. history found that legislators have proposed solutions that include arming teachers, adding guards or police officers, and shoring up the security of school buildings." Predictably, the proposed bills mirror the school safety recommendations made by field experts. Not a single bill targeted improving administrative discretion in high-stakes decision-making, nor was a bill proposed to target efforts to bring forward increased inter-rater reliability that would produce more consistent data reporting about school violence and perhaps lead to discovery of root causes.

Empirical evidence is seldom included in proposed school safety bills. Of the 450 proposed bills, sixty-two sought safety upgrades, including eliminating or reducing the size of windows in schools (Shah & Ujifusa, 2014).

However, eliminating or reducing the size of windows contradicts the findings of studies that linked student performance to exposure to natural light. In 1999, the Heschong Mahone Group study of thousands of classrooms across multiple states found that "children who took their lessons in classrooms with more natural light scored up to 25% higher on standardized tests than other students in the same school" (Heschong Mahone Group, 1999).

Shah and Ujifusa (2014) identify forty-four of the bills as being specific to gun control, despite the lack of benefits derived from the passage of the 1990 Gun-Free School Zones Act. This point is further elaborated by Daniel Webster, director of the Center for Gun Policy and Research at Johns Hopkins University, who adds that "schools might be a likely target because that is where a mass of people congregate and those people involve a lot of troubled adolescents who may harbor bad feelings toward the people there who bullied them, were unfair to them, etc. The shooters in these instances didn't say, 'Hey, I'll find a gun-free zone where I can shoot a lot of people.' No, they went to a place for reasons wholly unrelated to gun-free zones" (Berry, 2013).

Chapter Twenty-Eight

Bollards and Planters

The Terrible Ideas That Are Coming to a School Near You

Bollards are an antiterrorism measure intended to protect cities and schools from a new breed of terrorist: the vehicle striker. Remember in 2016 when someone drove a truck over all those pedestrians as they walked down the lovely Mediterranean seafront in Nice, France? Or the copycat crime that then struck London? Bollards are supposed to end this little spree. They're these stupid, often grotesquely overpriced, mammoth tusk–like posts that school officials like to sink into the cement in front of school doors (and windows and random objects) in the hopes that they will stop future terrorists intent on driving cars into things and save our kids from . . .

Unfortunately, no one seems to notice how bad the logic is. Security vendors recommend planting bollards all over everything in the schoolyard, like the school is an hors d'oeuvre tray and they're covering it with tooth-picks. This is partly because it's an emotionally charged topic—so, as with the metal detectors, people latch onto expensive fixes that sound nice and concrete without giving them a lot of thought.

Sure, bollard proponents can cite plenty of instances in which persons intentionally used vehicles to mow down pedestrians on walking paths. Such was the case on October 31, 2017. Eight people were killed when Sayfullo Saipov used a rented pickup truck to strike cyclists and runners on a Manhattan bike path (Yan & Andone, 2017).

Bollards have been deployed in the fight against terrorism for several years—mainly around population-dense areas such as arenas and stadiums—but the Nice and London truck attacks have fast-tracked the process to a ridiculous degree. Bollards are popping up across the world like an elephant graveyard slowly emerging from sandy soil. They are now largely standard fixtures for new school buildings, at least in front of the main entrance, and are included as retrofits to existing buildings.

A search for "bollards" on Amazon returned hundreds of options. Some were even marketed as a hybrid of artwork and bollard: a little sculpture to plant in front of your school that's also supposed to stop a truck full of fertilizer. Some schools paint them up to look like oversized pencils sticking out of the pavement—cute, but it's just a hat on a bad hair day.

Bollards aren't the only goofy obstacle you can spend money on; you can also get a highly decorative, three-thousand-pound cement flower planter barrier.

They look particularly postapocalyptic in the winter (and it's unnerving how many of these things resemble open caskets—even an eighty-five-year-old retired librarian made that observation when out for a Sunday drive). To use another World War II comparison, our schoolyards now look like the beaches of Normandy on the eve of D-Day, bristling with contraptions sticking out of the ground.

And how did that defense work out for the Germans? It's unchecked insanity, but it's visible, and that's what parents want—safety they will see, safety they can touch or kick with a foot. It's concrete; so what if it doesn't work?

However, can you point to a school safety assessment that used any evidence to rank bollards or flower planters in the top tier of priorities? Good luck. A comprehensive safety assessment conducted by an unbiased safety expert (not a vendor) will always place communication systems, youth mental health, and threat input identification and reporting systems before bollards.

The reality is that nobody is going to drive a vehicle through the front doors of a school, even if they wanted to. The door to one local school that stuck one in there was already surrounded by a stumpy, pillared portico; *maybe* a professional driver could aim a Gremlin in there, if he was lucky. The bollards looked protective, but they were "protecting" the students from a near-impossible occurrence while mopping up funds that could have gone to something useful. More terrorism benchmarking: "If it happened there, it can happen here."

If anything, they're going to cause injuries. How would you like to be a student on crutches, or in a wheelchair, navigating that portico? They will also make it harder to shovel in front of the main door during winter, allowing melted snow to refreeze and create more slippery patches.

Yeah, icy areas by the main entrances of buildings—hmmm. Meanwhile, take a look at the wide-open sidewalk in front of these bollards. Another school nearby widened the sidewalk in the back of the building to make it easier to stage students for their bus pickups at the end of the day. That sidewalk is about the width of a truck, and there isn't a bollard in sight. It's almost as though they only take preventative measures when they are convenient and look good. Today's safety solutions that are not well considered could become tomorrow's safety problems.

Bollards work in that they stop vehicles. But as a fortification measure, they fall short unless you wrap these things around every building, every playground, and so on, which is counterproductive in some laughably predictable ways. Well, it isn't so funny if you die. Peppering bike paths with bollards has resulted in documented deaths and severe injuries from riders who have collided with the intrusive features, especially at night.

In his article "The Trail Bollard Hazard," experienced bicyclist Pete Medek describes the damage bollards can do. "I've had a friend die from injuries he suffered as a result of a bollard crash. Another friend was riding with her brother, who also died from bollard crash injuries. I rode upon the scene of another bollard crash that bloodied a young man's face, and of course I had my close call . . . all on the same trail" (Medek, 2012).

So why are perceptive cyclists, like Medek, crashing into bollards? Here's one reason: per the Federal Highway Administration (U.S. Department of Transportation, Federal Highway Administration, 2018), "Bollards

Figure 28.1. Wisconsin elementary school with newly installed safety bollards, 2018. *Credit: David Perrodin.*

are involved in 'second user' crashes, where the first user hides the bollard until it is too late to avoid it, even if the first user has adequate sight distance. These crashes can produce serious or incapacitating injuries. This can happen to pedestrians as well as bicyclists or other higher speed users."

So by all means we would want an emergency vehicle to cleanly travel over a public recreation path. What if a jogger collapsed? What if a roller-blader dodged a squirrel and tumbled her way to a fractured leg? Try to imagine speed-walking rescuers weaving a stretcher between sets of bollards and onlookers.

Hopefully, the paramedics played plenty of Frogger when they were kids or read books about the sea and hawk-eyed barrelman in the crow's nest yelling the locations of rocky formations off the starboard side. See how "solving" one problem that really wasn't a problem to start with creates a cascade effect of new, real problems?

And had bollards been in place on the sidewalks at the Murrah Building in Oklahoma City, the bomb-laden truck would have just been parked a few feet further away on the road, and the building would have still endured the same damage that rocked the entire neighborhood.

These devices won't deter school shooters. Ultimately, you harden one location and shift the attacker's emphasis to other, lesser-fortified locations—and there are many, from bus pickups to playgrounds to the packed-house outdoor bleachers customary on Friday nights in the United States. It's amazing, frankly, that a school shooter hasn't targeted a football stadium, as it provides a target-dense mass with few escape routes and no cover, and darkness would certainly be an advantage to the shooter lurking beyond the far fences.

Remember: You can't fortify your way to school safety. The key to reducing threats and interrupting threats is intelligence, or threat identification and reporting, which we do a very underwhelming job of in schools, even though schools will rush in to show off their nifty app-based reporting system. When you think of threat identification, images of gigantic 1930s "war tubas" come to mind (they look as menacingly amusing as they sound, but you'll want to do an image search on Google anyway). These goofy sound collection contraptions were an attempt to suck in and analyze sound from the sky; before radar, the best way to detect enemy planes was to listen for their noises. By detecting roaring engines at greater distances, one was allowed more time to prepare a response.

Same with schools—we would be better off trying to detect threats than installing more bulletproof windows. Many school attacks have been prevented by the investigation of reported threats that led to the discovery of arsenals and plans. These "near misses" don't make the headlines, though—nor are they diligently recorded in a uniform database. But by all accounts we should be investing a larger share of our safety resources on the threat identification side as our student population grows more diverse by the day; for many, identifying and reporting threats involves overcoming language and communication barriers.

How about students with disabilities or limited English language skills who struggle to comprehend safety instructions or don't adequately understand how threat reporting works? Per the National Center for Educational Statistics, "In 2015–16, the number of students ages 3–21 receiving special education services was 6.7 million, or 13 percent of all public school students. Among students receiving special education services, 34 percent had specific learning disabilities per the Individuals with Disabilities Education Act" (National Center for Educational Statistics, 2018). These figures do not include millions more children with anxiety, depression, or mental health needs that do not receive special education services.

Educators think they are somehow "protecting" students with special needs by limiting their participation in safety drills. Many of these students present unique challenges during emergency situations, and they shouldn't just be included in regular safety planning; there should be specialized safety plans in place for them. And for those plans to be successful there needs to be preparation and practice.

We already mentioned the youth code of silence. September 11 resulted in massive threat detection measures—and sure, it's a rich debate on whether we've sacrificed personal privacy for personal safety, but you can duke that out in constitutional chat forums.

Political backing for safe learning environments has engendered past and present school safety laws that appear to have been erected upon well-intentioned but empirically devoid public sentiment. Politicians are making public endorsements of safety strategies, such as having all students enter and exit a school through one set of doors, within a day or two of a school shooting. They feel pressured to say something, and invariably say the wrong thing. As Astor and Benbenishty (2005) observe, "Politicians frequently embrace the notion that students cannot learn when their schools are unsafe. In fact, national policy, such as No Child Left Behind, acknowledged this with the 'persistently dangerous school' clause, allowing parents to find a safer school if their child's school is deemed dangerous" (p. 52).

However, we now face a combination of narrow definitions, high thresholds, and reluctance to report events. Nowadays, parents shop for schools via open enrollment, and a school with high suspension numbers is not perceived as a safe school—so kids who make threats are swept under the carpet. Student recruitment includes billboards and television commercials. There is much pressure and incentive to suppress authentic threat reporting as declining enrollment is the death knell of a public school district funded by headcounts. Most states report that they do not have any persistently dangerous schools (Astor & Benbenishty, 2005, p.52). It is clear that laws based on an already broken system of reporting that almost forces those reporting the data to cheat to stay employed can't work.

North Carolina's 2015–2016 guide on how to report discipline data contained at least 114 student behaviors that could be reported on, including gambling and affray (an affray is two or more people fighting in public). Gambling—really? Just because you can collect the data doesn't mean you should collect the data. There is little interterminology reliability from state to state and aggregated data at the federal level are contaminated beyond any useful application (Perrodin, 2015).

For a teacher or administrator who isn't a researcher, how are you supposed to parse all of this out? It might sound suspiciously folksy, but when research can't be trusted you might have to—or even want to—rely on common sense and heuristics. A good rule of thumb is: If it sounds like it's being done to make people feel like they're doing something, look for another solution. Often modest tweaks, although they might not be the kind of stuff that launches great media-friendly programs, are more effective than big projects.

Even small tech-based safety improvements should be thought of in terms of what works rather than what makes parents and administrators feel good. As we have seen, general systems advances in technology (cell phone systems that can handle a surge) tend to add more to safety than localized gadgets (metal detectors and high-definition cameras); this has been proven often enough that it makes sense to advise schools to work within systems as they develop instead of trying to create new ones. So schools that develop their own safety app are wasting time and money on something that will *never* become a core part of their students' online life; it's both school related (*lame!*) and specific to a kind of event kids never want to contemplate in advance.

Schools are designed to deliver and inculcate, shoving rules and information down kids' throats. It's a one-way street that is fine when it comes to teaching them things they don't know that they don't know, but as a steady diet—especially when it comes to safety—it paralyzes them.

Focus groups take them out of that paralysis and help receive the students' ideas and use them to inform your practices and systems. Remember, systems develop, but you can do things to smooth that process. Find out from the kids how to tie into their trusted social media tribe. This is one of the reasons focus groups are such an amazing tool: they let you *ask the kids themselves* these questions, both so that you get a real answer instead of a clueless adult trying to guess and also to dissolve the code of silence.

Then, when a disaster strikes, you don't need them to go to an app or seek you out. In flailing on their phones, they will get to your safety info, no matter how panicked they are. As we've seen before, their tribe is their telephone; by injecting centralized information into that tribe you will give them more decision-making power. This is a slice of normalcy that will give them a lifeline and help funnel them toward optimal solutions.

Chapter Twenty-Nine

A Mile Wide and an Inch Deep

There is one lesson that the safety experts in NYC seem to have learned very well after 9/11: prioritization is all about probability, or the likelihood of a given event's occurrence.

After the 9/11 Lower Manhattan boat rescue, NYC didn't create a fleet of harbor rescue boats, mandate harbor evacuation drills, or require high-rises to be encased in impenetrable exoskeletons. They realized that 9/11 is a statistical outlier.

They don't practice in Battery Park these days because they don't expect another harbor evacuation. Other city governments seem to understand this as well; you don't see the architecture tour boats in Chicago drilling in front of Millennial Park every year just in case lightning strikes the exact same way it did in New York.

Safety officials in cities are more concerned with the overall systems: What do we do for backup when the telecable system fails, for instance? We wish more schools would understand this.

Instead, most schools go with the "Mile Wide and Inch Deep Theory of Safety," making specific fixes for a million highly improbable scenarios instead of fixing big picture problems like situational awareness, torus expansion, improving access to safety education and threat reporting for all students, deciphering the youth code of silence, and drill fidelity. Largely this is because they fail to understand the word "improbable"—or more likely, because the parents don't understand it, and they treat the parents like customers whose every wish is their command.

You're the experts, guys, not the parents! We should treat the parents with respect as human beings, but for Pete's sake, as a profession, we need to remember that this is not their specialty, no matter how emotionally tied up they are in their kids' safety, and stop letting them drive the car. It's frightening to have brain surgery. That doesn't mean it will come out better if your nervous brother screams instructions at the surgeon while you're on the operating table.

Probability particularly eludes helicopter parents—the type who like to squash their kid's bagel into a mini doughnut hole; any probability that isn't zero means it's time to press the panic button. The panic button is, typically, directly connected to the school's budget, and they expect it to spew out cash in response.

For example, one mother pressured her school district to put a staff member on her child's bus, someone trained in identifying symptoms of anaphylactic reaction and capable of administering an epinephrine shot. Her argument was that her son was a high-risk candidate for a life-threatening reaction to a bee sting, and if a bee flew through a bus window and stung him, EMTs might not reach him in time to save his life.

Whoa. The odds of a bee flying onto the bus, stinging this kid, and then killing him before the safety systems that were already in place could get him help in time were astronomically low.

And this would set a precedent that would open the door to fund a staff member on each bus just in case a child had a reaction or medical event. For the tiny probability that somehow the entire medical response system was going to decide to break down at the exact moment a bee flew in a window and made a line for her kid, she was willing to demand that the community cough up for an entire extra staffing position. And if she got through the gate, everyone else whose child had a nonzero possibility of ever dying would want a staffer too. It's enough to make anyone want to pull out their hair.

How to deal with this kind of demand? All you can do is remember that *you're the expert*, so instead of focusing on customer service, provide evidence and stay calm and professional. Unfortunately, sometimes other professionals are all too willing to get sucked into the helicopter parents' whirling blades, so you have to be ready to deal with that too.

In this case, first, district officials met with the bus company and the local ambulance service and were assured that the bus, which had a GPS transponder on it, would be reached in a timely manner by emergency responders on the typical routes to school and back home. Now, nothing is failsafe, but this made sense.

The school's business manager went a step further and contacted the school's lawyer. That was a big mistake. The lawyer was unwilling to give an immediate opinion and came back a day later. She had a story from another state a few years ago when a child had an anaphylactic reaction on a bus and died. Hence, the lawyer's position was: "Well, it's not likely, but it could happen—so you have to decide how much risk you"—by which she meant the school district—"are willing to take on." Thanks for nothing, lady! Classic "Mile Wide, Inch Deep" thinking: well, it happened once somewhere on the planet and a mom is loudly worried about it, so let's stick this expensive, piecemeal solution into our safety system and see how that works out.

Takeaway: Don't go to the district's lawyer for anything but purely legal questions. Lawyers are lousy assessors of safety risks and will always go off and dig up scenarios or options, but they leave it up to you to pick what is behind door number two. If they work for the district, as this lady did, they may well be invested in doing the customer service tap dance for the parents as well. Lawyers are not experts in school safety, industrial safety, or rescues. They know law—and the expert witness takes care of the content matter.

Chapter Thirty

Final Implications for School Leaders

So you've made it to the end of the explanations and evidence. And now your faith is shaken in specific plans. But there are overarching statements that can be helpful in future safety initiatives; it's not all about pure situational awareness and systems that will develop. If you're like most in the safety field, and you want to make sure you do your job right in the future, you've probably been hoping this book will end with some firm takeaways.

LEADING AND PLANNING

1. A little leadership goes a long way.
2. Too often we develop linear plans for what will be nonlinear events. For example, a natural gas leak is identified in the school. Per the existing safety plan, the off-campus evacuation site is two blocks away. The fire department issues a six-block evacuation radius. Now what? You need your staff to be able to look at uncertainty and not lose their minds.
3. Contingency planning must include and staunchly support discretion and improvisation to act in the best interests of others and self. Attempting to script response protocols for virtually unimaginable events is not effective as the response plan won't match the scenario. We also overlook that contexts and situations naturally evolve over time, as demonstrated by the rapid advances in cellular and Internet technologies in the past twenty years.
4. Don't benchmark schools to other schools or school incidents to other school incidents.
5. Run-hide-fight is the traditional intruder mantra. A better idea would be Embrace, Assess, Inventory, and Decide. People are more likely to

defend themselves after being explicitly told, "If you feel that your life or the lives of students are at immediate risk, then do whatever you deem necessary to stay alive, including throwing things at an intruder or striking the intruder." People accept risks when facing prospects of loss but avoid risks when facing prospects of gain.

6. Be flexible to interface with new resources. Remember how the Zello app enabled Cajun Navy Relief to rescue people impacted by flooding? Here's one more example of how technology recasts emergency response platforms. Launched in 2013, the global addressing system "what3words" has divided the world into a grid of three meter by three meter squares and assigned each one a permanent, unique three-word address. There are so many practical uses for this kind of technology. For instance, in a crisis situation, it could guide parents to a specific entrance of the impromptu student-parent "reunification" building a mile away from the school.

7. Conveying information to rescuers and the public is essential. This was managed well during 9/11 by New York City mayor Rudy Giuliani's press conferences.

AWARENESS AND INDUCTION

1. Rescue is compromised by those coming to the scene to check on others but are not part of the rescue effort. This actually wasn't an issue on 9/11 as the civilians were not allowed access to Lower Manhattan and therefore didn't add to the congestion—the rescuers could do their jobs without having to navigate crowds of relatives or onlookers. But it has been a big deal elsewhere. Parents, relatives, curious folk, self-dispatched responders, and media rushing to Columbine (1999) and Sandy Hook (2012), clogging essential routes to the site. Some simply bolted from their vehicles, abandoning them in the middle of streets, and ran toward the school.

2. Host an evening assembly a week prior to the start of the school year to tell the parents and community members what to anticipate during and following a crisis. This is known as priming and is very effective in helping people handle crisis events. (Record the presentation so it can be an induction tool!) Explain that if a reunification site is necessary, it will be determined as part of "working the problem" of the event.

3. With attrition and turnover in mind, what is the induction process for staff and students that join the school after the traditional start-of-year safety training? We have to work to keep knowledge in the institution from year to year, and also within years. Distributed leadership was

present in schools years ago but can no longer be counted on due to frequent turnover of leaders, staff, and transient students.

THE PSYCHOLOGY OF SAFETY

1. Explain chaos and identify that the introduction of "noise" into a situation can actually simplify decision-making by reducing options. This also includes describing the torus and self-similarity.
2. Negotiating suboptimal solutions can incrementally get you to a safer place.
3. Are we teaching situational awareness and sensemaking?
4. The transference dynamic was a significant factor contributing to the success of the harbor rescue. How does the modern school administrator account for the transference dynamic that might influence reactions of staff and students? Today, he or she might place trust in technology during a rescue versus trust in a system or in others. This is often the argument with the millennial generation—that they tend to operate better in horizontal organizations than vertical organizations and perhaps operate best almost as independent contractors of their services.

DRILLS

1. Drill fatigue, including student apathy and becoming desensitized, are documented in research studies. Many schools throughout the United States are mandated to hold drills, or operational exercises, to prepare for fires, tornadoes, violence, and other emergencies. Despite recommendations by the Federal Emergency Management Agency and US-DOE, no local or federal agency routinely monitors the frequency and quality of school drills. Hence, drills are often checklist activities and not exercises to better inform practice.
2. Interagency drills have limitations. In practice, interagency drills are multiagency drills. If a school intruder event happened a day following such a drill, expect a different set of responders from those who participated in the drill. Also, expect turnover, attrition, change in tools, and changes in practices over time, and put genuine methods of preserving knowledge in place. Quarterly tabletop exercises allow essential actors to practice making decisions during crisis situations.
3. Weather and time of day influence crisis response and rescues. School safety drills tend to be on 9/11 type days—perfect weather and in the morning. Drill as the buses arrive at school, at lunch, and at recess. Include all students in all drills.

4. Periodically extending drills beyond their typical durations will help staff and students experience moving from the center of their torus and toward a less-explored portion of the bagel.

Epilogue

Nothing Means Anything to Anyone Until It Means
Everything to You

Even when drills are conducted with fidelity, another phenomenon that takes a toll is systems fatigue; this is why New York City adopted a measured approach to physical structure security following the September 11, 2001, attacks. Systems fatigue happens when personnel are overwhelmed by the demands required to sustain safety models.

A school administrator approached the threat reporting software representative with a common dilemma. The district's threat input system (bullying, harassment, harm to self or others) was abundantly utilized by students—and most of the bullying reports, for example, could not be substantiated by evidence.

Schools have finite resources, and a single comprehensive investigation of a threat might require hours of interviewing students, reviewing posts to social media, and so on. It's reasonable that a school district would want to streamline its threat reporting and threat investigation processes because principals have their plates full.

Therein lies the rub. The system was working, and it was overworking the staff. In fact, an assistant principal resigned after a grueling year that included personally investigating and documenting more than one hundred reported threats with ninety dismissed due to lack of evidence or determination that the threat was valid. But here's the catch: the students reporting the threats perceived them, we will assume, as authentic incidents.

We also have to work with the allowances of frontal lobe development, hormones, and such, so the kids probably aren't attempting to sabotage the reporting system. The term "bullying" has been overused and incorrectly applied to the degree that it has muddied the reporting waters. The default position for school officials, often per requirement of state laws or local policies, is that a report of bullying is regarded as bullying until proven to not be bullying.

A typical playground conflict between two kids that each wanted to be the pitcher in a game of kickball must be scrutinized as a potential bullying incident. Things like that sometimes take hours to resolve and one parent was convinced that her child was the recipient of bullying and aired that grievance on social media with a scathing comment on the school's page as well as her personal page.

The district representative directed me to recommend additional layers to the front end of the threat input system—additional "filters" to sift out the reports that probably wouldn't be substantiated by evidence through a formal investigation. You know what I'm talking about—the annoying "pop-up" boxes that appear with, "Are you *sure* you want to submit this?" Deterrent boxes. The district would pony up the dollars for an overhauled system for MERV-16-level filtration so fewer referrals made it to the principal's inbox. The thought of an obstacle course came to mind.

The existing system appeared to be fine-tuned; there wasn't a clanging noise or obvious flat tire. Perhaps the fundamental challenges of this situation will be better revealed through this parallel illustration. Most of the time a school fire alarm tab is pulled by accident or as a prank.

But what if fire alarms were different? What if the person that activated the alarm was required to stand in place and bark into an intercom speaker in order to "authenticate" the alarm? So, pretend a voice crackles over the fire alarm speaker and asks, "What is your name?" Pause. "Why did you pull the alarm?" Pause. Cough. "What color is the smoke?" Pause. Cough. Wipe sweat from brow (sure is getting hot in here).

"Describe the odor—is it like when something electrical is burning?" and so on. Ridiculous, right? We don't shift the investigation to the reporter, but that's covertly what this school district thought needed to happen to prevent their investigation-scrambling principals from burning out. (And as this paragraph smolders, it would be prudent to consider bringing students with disabilities from the sidelines of safety and center them to active roles of detecting and reporting threats.)

So we had a rather difficult meeting. Upon due diligence of examining the reporting system, I informed the district representative that I could not justify modifications to the existing model as such changes would make the system less accessible to students. Well, that was a short chitchat. The district folks believed (or hoped) that the threat input system could be modified and maintain fidelity. I wasn't in alignment with that hypothesis, and so I was thanked and given notice that our partnership would be over at month's end. Business is business, but in school safety, it's never as simple as that. Lives are in the balance. I was disappointed as this was a decision driven by personnel—it wasn't personal, but kind of felt that way.

Two weeks later I received a call. Upon further study and reflection, the district changed course and decided to maintain its threat input system and allocate more people to investigate threat reports. Good move. The representative expressed appreciation that I stated what the "brass" *needed* to hear, not what they *wanted* to hear. Hey, I'm not here to sell you metal detectors. I was invited to continue safety consulting with the school district. This is the real story: even when a safety system is working well, it's the human component that can fatigue, but a true safety professional always acts in the interest of staff and students, even if that means losing the cash.

References

Astor, R. A., & Benbenishty, R. (2005). Zero tolerance for zero knowledge [Commentary]. *Education Week*, pp. 24, 52.

Baden-Powell, R. (2018). Scouting games (unknown earlier versions). U.S. Scouting Services. Retrieved from http://www.macscouter.com/Games/bp_chapter2.asp#Heading57.

Baumeister, R. F., Chesner, S. P., Senders, P. S., & Tice, D. M. (1988). Who's in charge here? Group leaders do lend help in emergencies. *Personality and Social Psychology Bulletin, 14*(1), 17–22. Retrieved from http://dx.doi.org/10.1177/0146167288141002.

Begley, P., & Stefkovich, J. (2007). Ethical school leadership: Defining the best interests of students. *Educational Management Administration & Leadership*, *35*(2), 214. SAGE Publications.

Berry, J. (2013, January 17). Examining the last 20 years of mass shootings through the lens of "gun free" zones. Retrieved from http://www.nashuatelegraph.com/news/990499-469/examining-the-last-20-years-of-mass.html#.

Bloom, H. K. (1997). The Lucifer principle: A scientific expedition into the forces of history. *Atlantic Monthly Press*.

Bloom, H. (2012). *The God problem: how a godless cosmos creates*. Amherst, NY: Prometheus Books.

Casner, S., Geven, R., & Williams, K. (2013, June). The effectiveness of airline pilot training for abnormal events. *Human Factors*, *55*(3), p. 477.

Centers for Disease Control and Prevention. (2009). School connectedness: Strategies for increasing protective factors among youth. Atlanta, GA: U.S. Department of Health and Human Services. Retrieved from https://www.cdc.gov/healthyyouth/protective/pdf/connectedness.pdf.

Cohen, F., Solomon, S., Maxfield, M., Pyszczynski, T., & Greenberg, J. (2004, December). Fatal attraction: The effects of mortality salience on evaluations of charismatic, task-oriented, and relationship-oriented leaders. *Psychol Sci.* (12), pp. 846–51. PubMed PMID: 15563330.

Davis, B. (2016). *Marine!: The life of Chesty Puller*. Open Road Media.

Dedman, B. (2006). Does every school need a metal detector? *NBC News*. Retrieved from http://www.nbcnews.com/id/15111439/ns/us_news-crime_and_courts/t/does-every-school-need-metal-detector/#.W4gdwOhKiUl.

Derbyshire, D. (2007, June 15). How children lost the right to roam in four generations. *Daily Mail. U.K.* Retrieved from http://www.dailymail.co.uk/news/article-462091/How-children-lost-right-roam-generations.html.

Dunkirk Evacuation. (Editors of Encyclopedia Britannica). (2018, May 19). Encyclopedia Britannica. Retrieved from https://www.britannica.com/event/Dunkirk-evacuation.

Fox News. (2017, December 27). Army and Homeland Security prepping teachers for the gunman at the door. Retrieved from http://www.foxnews.com/us/2017/12/27/army-and-homeland-security-prepping-teachers-for-gunman-at-door.html.

Garcia-Navarro, L. (Host). (2017, November 19). School trip to D.C. canceled over fears of mass shooting. [Radio broadcast episode]. National Public Radio. Retrieved from https://www.npr.org/2017/11/19/565153406/school-trip-to-d-c-canceled-over-fears-of-mass-shooting.

Garger, K., Rachman, C., & O'Neill, N. (2016). Airhead teen busted for climbing World Trade Center rises again. *New York Post*. Retrieved from https://nypost.com/2016/11/27/airhead-teen-busted-for-climbing-world-trade-center-rises-again/.

Garner, B. A., (Ed.) (2009). *Black's law dictionary*. (Sixth edition). St. Paul, MN: Thomas Reuters.

Heschong Mahone Group. (1999). An investigation into the relationship between daylighting and human performance. Retrieved from http://www.h-m-g.com/downloads/Daylighting/schoolc.pdf.

Hobbes, T. (1969). *Leviathan, 1651*. Menston: Scolar P.

Internet World Stats. (2018). Internet growth statistics. Retrieved from https://www.internetworldstats.com/emarketing.htm.

Ma, A. (2018, May 8). Anxiety over shootings bolsters $2.7 billion school security industry. *Marketplace*. Retrieved from https://www.marketplace.org/2018/05/08/education/anxiety-over-shootings-bolsters-27-billion-school-security-industry.

Martinell, TJ. (2018, March 17). Rituals make us stronger. Interview with TJ Martinell. *The Safety Doc Podcast*. Retrieved from http://safetyphd.com/safety-doc-podcast-63-rituals-make-us-stronger-interview-with-tj-martinell/.

McAllister Towing and Transportation Co., Inc. (2018). About McAllister > History. Retrieved from https://www.mcallistertowing.com/AboutMcAllister/History.aspx.

McCann, S. J. (1992). Alternative formulas to predict the greatness of U.S. presidents: Personological, situational, and zeitgeist factors. *Journal of Personality and Social Psychology, 62*(3), pp. 469–79. http://dx.doi.org/10.1037/0022-3514.62.3.469.

Medek, P. (2012, June 13). The Trail Bollard Hazzard. Ohio Bikeways. Retrieved from https://www.ohiobikeways.net/bollard_hazard.htm.

National Center for Educational Statistics. (2018, April). Children and youth with disabilities. Retrieved from https://nces.ed.gov/programs/coe/indicator_cgg.asp.

National Policy Board for Educational Administration. (2015). *Professional standards for educational leaders 2015*. Reston, VA: Author.

Perrodin, D. (2013, May. 22). School security and crisis preparedness. [Television broadcast]. Madison, WI: Wisconsin Public Television. Retrieved from https://video.wpt.org/video/university-place-school-security-and-crisis-preparedness/.

Perrodin, D. (2015, December 23). David Perrodin, school safety expert discusses the importance of new data requirements from the Office for Civil Rights. Sprigeo. Santa Barbara, CA. Retrieved from https://sprigeo.com/expert-interviews/1713/.

Perrodin, D. (2017, January 7). Three spectacular in-the-moment high-stakes decisions that saved lives. *The Safety Doc Podcast*. Retrieved from http://safetyphd.com/three-spectacular-in-the-moment-high-stakes-decisions-that-saved-lives-sdp9/.

Pechon, K. (2017, October 1). Cajun Navy insider—Katie Pechon interview—True untold stories. *The Safety Doc Podcast*. Retrieved from http://safetyphd.com/cajun-navy-insider-katie-pechon-interview-true-untold-stories-sdp46/.

Popejoy, C. (2018). Troy Polamalu impostor sneaks into Steelers practice, says he wants to cover Antonio Brown. *USA Today*. Retrieved from https://www.usatoday.com/story/sports/nfl/steelers/2018/08/11/steelers-troy-polamalu-impostor-sneaks-into-practice-antonio-brown/111229724/.

Ramirez, M., Kubicek, K., Peek-Asa, C., & Wong, M. (2009). Accountability and assessment of emergency drill performance at schools. *Family & Community Health, 32*(2), pp. 105–14.

Riecker, T. (2018). ICS: Who doesn't need it? Exploring emergency management and Homeland Security. Retrieved from https://triecker.wordpress.com/2016/02/10/ics-who-doesnt-need-it/.

Ripley, A. (2008). *The unthinkable: Who survives when disaster strikes and why.* New York: Crown Publishers.

Roediger, H. L., & Finn, B. (2010). The pluses of getting it wrong. *Scientific American Mind, 21*(1), 33-35. Retrieved from http://psychnet.wustl.edu/memory/wp-content/uploads/2018/04/Roediger-Finn-2010_SAM.pdf.

Rosenstein, E. (2011). *Boatlift* [Motion picture]. Eyepop Productions. Retrieved from https://www.youtube.com/watch?v=MDOrzF7B2Kg.

Salvo, J. J., Lobo, A. P., & Alvarez, J. A. (2007). A pre- and post-9/11 look (2000–2005) at Lower Manhattan. Population Division, New York City Department of City Planning.

Shah, N., & Ujifusa, A. (2014, October 29). School safety legislation since Newtown. *Edweek.* Retrieved from http://www.edweek.org/ew/section/multimedia/school-safety-bills-since-newtown.html.

Sherif, M., Harvey, O. J., White, B. J., Hood, W. E., & Sherif, C. S. (1961). *Intergroup conflict and cooperation: The Robbers Cave experiment.* Norman: University of Oklahoma Book Exchange.

Spillane, J. P. (2005). Distributed leadership. *The Educational Forum, 69,* p. 146.

Spillane, J. P., & Orlina, E. C. (2005). Investigating leadership practice: Exploring the entailments of taking a distributed perspective. *Leadership & Policy in Schools, 4*(3), p. 158. doi: 10.1080/15700760500244728.

Stefkovich, J. A., & O'Brien, M. (2004). Best interests of the student: An ethical model. *Journal of Educational Administration* (42), pp. 197–214.

Trump, K. (2015). 5 reasons metal detectors in schools are a bad idea, according to security expert. Retrieved from https://www.masslive.com/news/index.ssf/2015/05/5_reasons_metal_detectors_in_school_are_bad.html.

U.S. Department of Transportation, Federal Highway Administration. (2018). *Bollards, gates and other barriers.* Retrieved from https://www.fhwa.dot.gov/environment/recreational_trails/guidance/bollards_access.cfm.

U.S. Federal Bureau of Investigation. (2000). The school shooter: A threat assessment perspective. p. 1. Retrieved from https://www.fbi.gov/file-repository/stats-services-publications-school-shooter-school-shooter/view.

U.S. Federal Emergency Management Agency. (2018, March). *IS-139.A: Exercise design and development.* Emergency Management Institute. Retrieved from https://training.fema.gov/is/courseoverview.aspx?code=IS-139.a.

U.S. Federal Emergency Management Agency. (2015, December). *IS-907: Active shooter: What you can do.* Emergency Management Institute. Retrieved from https://training.fema.gov/is/courseoverview.aspx?code=IS-907.

U.S. Secret Service and U.S. Department of Education. (2008). *Prior knowledge of potential school-based violence: Information students learn may prevent a targeted attack.* Washington, DC, p. 6. Retrieved from http://www.doe.in.gov/sites/default/files/safety/bystander-study.pdf.

Van Vugt, M., & De Cremer, D. (1999). Leadership in social dilemmas: The effects of group identification on collective actions to provide public goods. *Journal of Personality and Social Psychology, 76*(4), pp. 587–99. Retrieved from http://dx.doi.org/10.1037/0022-3514.76.4.587.

Van Vugt, M., Hogan, R., & Kaiser, R. B. (2008). Leadership, followership, and evolution: Some lessons from the past. *American Psychologist, 63*(3), 189. Retrieved from http://dx.doi.org/10.1037/0003-066X.63.3.182.

Varian, F. (2013, April 28). A 40-year veteran of the telecom industry and crisis communications profession offers his opinions about analog versus digital 2-way radios relative to school security. [Blog post]. Retrieved from http://safetyphd.com/exclusive-interview-a-40-year-veteran-of-the-telecom-industry-and-crisis-communications-profession-offers-his-opinions-about-analog-versus-digital-2-way-radios-relative-to-school-security/.

Weick, K. E. (1995). *Sensemaking in organizations.* Thousand Oaks, CA: Sage.

Weick, K., Sutcliffe, K., & Obstfeld, D. (2005). Organizing the process of sensemaking. *Organizational Science, 16*(4), p. 409.

Williams, R., & Williams G. (2012, March 5). The use of social media for disaster recovery. University of Missouri Extension. Retrieved from http://joplintornado.info/joplin_documents/Using%20Social%20Media%20for%20Disasters.pdf.

Wunderground. (2001). September 11, 2001 weather forecast for Central Park, New York. Retrieved from https://www.wunderground.com/history/airport/KNYC/2001/9/11/Daily-History.html.

Yan, H., & Andone, D. (2017, November 2). Who is New York terror suspect Sayfullo Saipov? *CNN*. Retrieved from https://www.cnn.com/2017/11/01/us/sayfullo-saipov-new-york-attack/index.html.

Index

AARs. *See* After Action Reports
acceptable tolerances, 21
"Accountability and Assessment of Emergency Drills at School," 64
active shooter drills: absurdity of, 63; danger simulation in, trouble with, 65; focus of, misplaced, 1; limitations of, 40, 54; rubber bullets, 66
"Active Shooter: What You Can Do" course, 82–83
adaptability, 40
After Action Reports (AARs), 140
aggregation, 74–75
airplane pilot study, 132
airports: delays at, 106; metal detectors, 139–140
alphas, 45
Apollo 13, 106
Army, 81
assessment: insurance company, 7–9; of school drills, 64

Baden-Powell, Robert, 32
bagel metaphor. *See* the torus
benchmarking: bollards and, 146; definition of, 2, 49; generations in relation to, differences between, 50–51; Internet and, 55; lack of data for, 4–5; 9/11 and limitations of, 53–54, 56; paradox, 9; projected, 10–13; school safety and limitations of, 57

bias: in crisis analysis, 140; self-awareness of, 21–22; students best interests influenced by, 135; survey, 75
billion dollar industry, 1, 6–7
Bloom, Howard: Dawkins in relation to, 126, 127; on quantum physics, 17; superorganism concept of, 126
body politic, 126
bollards: benchmarking and, 146; as false deterrent, 148; as hazards, 146, 147–148; for school safety, 145–146, 147

Cajun Navy Relief: during Hurricane Harvey, 100; for Hurricane Katrina, forming of, 99–100; New York Harbor rescue in relation to, 101; Pechon working with, 100; social media and Zello helping, 100; spontaneity of, 141
Casner, Stephen, 132
cell phones: improvement of, 55–56, 139; on 9/11, use of, 95. *See also* smartphones
chaos: concentration during, 105; decision-making impacted by, 22–23; embracement of, 5; familiarity with, 131; flexibility of behavior in, 121; Hobbes on, 111–112; improvisation from, 106–107; liberation from, 106; motivation during, 122; paradox, 91; Puller's leadership in, 131;

169

sensemaking for functioning in, 29; social contracts holding up under, 112–113; unique response to, 106

chaos theory: biological analysis and, 142; Rapp as expert on, 119; simulated annealing in, 119, 120; the torus from, 2

Civil War, English, 110–111

Columbine school massacre, 94

comfort zone: exploration beyond, 25; flexibility and, 139; the torus regarding, 19

commercials, 21

communication: cell phones for, 55–56, 95, 139; interagency, 95; maritime radio for, 93, 95–96; in New York Harbor rescue, as key, 60; security, 95

Congress: Patriot Act passed by, 113–114; school safety bills and, 86

constructivism, 47

constructs: definition of, 74; as survey flaw, 75

contingency planning, 157

creative state, 122

Darwin, 125, 126

Dawkins: Bloom in relation to, 126, 127; leadership theory of, 125

The Day After, 50, 106

Department of Education, U.S., 76

Department of Homeland Security, 81

Derbyshire, David, 27

desensitization: of soldiers, 83; of students, 64

Dikkers, Seann: on shooter prevention, 84; on video games, 83–84

disaster: drills in relation to, 142; dynamics of, changing, 91; generations in relation to, differences between, 50–51; safety professionals adaptability during, 40; safety reassurance for parents following, 12; the torus regarding, 20, 23–24

discretion: improvisation linked to, 131–132; in-the-moment, 133; for leadership, 130; Loy empowering with, 131; situational, 78; of teachers, 134–135

distributed leadership: captains and crews demonstrating, 133–135; definition of, 130; faculty/staff lacking, 133; legacy knowledge in relation to, 130; of Loy, 10; turnover impacting, 158–159

distributed sensemaking, 133–135

district-level leadership, 86

drama drills, 64

drill buddy, 65

drill fatigue, 159

drill fidelity: guidelines for, 70–71; meaning of, 3; at School for the Blind, 60; teaching objectives for, 65

drills: AARs following, 140; active shooter, 1, 40, 54, 63, 65, 66; assessment of school, 64; disaster in relation to, 142; diversity for, 159–160; drama, 64; fire, 59–60, 63; interagency, 159; lockdown, 70; middle ground for, 73; qualitative information gathering after, 73–74; research on, poor quality, 63–64; situational awareness during, 30; for soldiers, 69; survey for faculty/staff following, 70–71; tabletop exercise, 77–78, 78, 79; tornado, 63; video games compared to, 82

drill trauma, 27

drones, 101

Dunkirk evacuation, 53–54

"The Effectiveness of Airline Pilot Training for Abnormal Events" study, 132

Emergency Management Institute, 96

empiricism, 47

EMS: ICS used by, 94; police coordinating with, 97, 98

endorsement: of Cajun Navy Relief, 100; of school fortification, 3

engagement: drill buddy for student, 65; qualitative information gathering for, 73–74; in simulated annealing, 121; surveys lack of, 76; tabletop exercise for, 78

English Civil War, 110–111

epistemology, 47

evolutionary leadership theories, 125–127

Exercise Design and Development course, 78

exploration: beyond comfort zone, 25; freedom for, lack of, 27; students denied, 26

Facebook, 99, 100
faculty/staff: bias of, 21–22; distributed
   leadership for, lack of, 133; drill survey
   for, 70–71; incident commander sought
   out by, 97, 98; ivory tower type, 85–86;
   safety presentation points for, 137–138;
   safety system development from, 92;
   threat reporting overworking, 161;
   transference dynamic influencing, 159.
   See also teachers
Federal Bureau of Investigation (FBI), 1, 5
Federal Emergency Management Agency
   (FEMA): "Active Shooter: What You
   Can Do" course, 82–83; Exercise
   Design and Development course, 78;
   Preparedness Branch, 96
field trips: benefits of, 27–28; parents fear
   of, 26; virtual, 27
fire drills: active shooter drills compared
   to, 63; at School for the Blind, 59–60
firefighters: ICS background for, 93–94;
   police coordinating with, 97, 98; at
   School for the Blind, 59
flexibility: of behavior in chaos, 121;
   comfort zone and, 139; discretion for
   teacher, 135; with technology, 158
flower planter barriers, 146
focus groups: qualitative information
   gathering in, 60, 73–74; for students,
   150
focus lock, 31, 31–32
followership, 125–126, 126
fortifications: false sense of security from,
   6; industry of school, 1; security
   failures of, 3–4
future preparation, 138

generalization, data, 75–76
geographic information system (GIS), 8
gun control legislation, 143
gut feelings: self-awareness in relation to,
   30; situational awareness and
   sensemaking for trusting, 29, 30;
   transference dynamic and, 44

heart rate variability, 142

helicopter parents: consequences from, 26,
   27, 154–155; probability eluding, 154
Heschong Mahone Group study, 143
Hobbes, T.: background on, 110; on chaos,
   111–112; English Civil War impacting,
   110–111; evolutionary leadership
   theorists compared to, 125–126; human
   nature observed by, 109; Machiavelli
   compared to, 110; on mankind's
   condition, 111; 9/11 in relation to, 110;
   philosophy of, 110; on power struggles
   and authority, 111–112; social contracts
   and, 112; the sovereign concept of, 112
Hoboken, 122
"hotwash," 77, 78
hurricanes: drones for, 101; Hurricane
   Harvey, 100; Hurricane Katrina,
   99–100

ICS. *See* Incident Command Structure
improvisation: from chaos, 106–107;
   discretion linked to, 131–132; of Loy,
   10; over protocols, 137
incident commander, 97, 98
Incident Command Structure (ICS):
   background on, 93–94; improvements
   to, 94–95; incident commander of, 97,
   98; on 9/11, problems with, 93, 94–95;
   Pechon and, 100–101; Riecker on, 96;
   for school shootings, 94; teachers and,
   96; Varian on, 95
individual responder research, 140–141
Individuals with Disabilities Education
   Act, 149
induction process, 158–159
instincts. *See* intuition/instincts
institutional memory: legacy knowledge
   compared to, 33–34; projected
   benchmarking and, 10–13
insurance company assessment, 7–9
interagency communication, 95
interagency drills, 159
Internet: benchmarking and, 55; legacy
   knowledge and, 129; Pechon on, 101.
   See also social media
interpretation, survey, 75
introspection, 139
intruder mantra, 142, 157

intuition/instincts: gut feelings and, 29, 30, 44; over planning, 3; Rapp on, 47; for safety systems, 3; unlearning bad habits for better, 117
ivory tower folks, 85–86

jargon, industry, 75
Joplin Tornado Information (JTI), 99

Kim's Game, 32

lawyers, 154–155
leadership: in chaos, Puller's, 131; discretion for, 130; distributed, 10, 130, 133–135, 158–159; evolutionary theories on, 125–127; followership and, 125–126, 126; natural, ability to recognize, 45–46; planning and, 157–158; PSEL and, 85, 86–87; Spillane on, 133; survival of the fittest at odds with, 126
leakage detection concept, 1
legacy knowledge: distributed leadership in relation to, 130; importance of, 129–130; institutional memory compared to, 33–34; Internet and, 129; the torus and, 34–35
legislators, 143
Leviathan (Hobbes): basis of, 109–110; English Civil War inspiration for, 110–111; on mankind's condition, 111
liberty: recovery of, 116; safety over, 113–114
lockdown drills, 70
Lower Manhattan: closing off of, 98; geography and demography of, 40–41, 41; lessons from, 2–5; uncertainty in, 105. *See also* New York Harbor rescue; 9/11
Loy, James: as alpha, 45; character of, 127; discretion of, for empowerment, 131; distributed leadership of, 10; on New York Harbor rescue, 13; safety system converging on, 119; as the sovereign, emerging, 113

Machiavelli, 110
Maginot Line, 6
mantra, safety, 5, 70, 142, 157–158

maritime radio, 93, 95–96
Martinell, TJ, 28
math, survivor, 113
Medek, Pete, 147
media: projected benchmarking from, 11; social, 13, 83, 99, 100
metal detectors: school, compared to airports, 139–140; uselessness of, 6–7
microaggressions, 46
Miller, Rory, 44
motivation: of Hobbes, 110; self-preservation as, 122
mountain peak analogy, 120

National Policy Board for Educational Administration (NPBEA), 85
New York Harbor rescue: Cajun Navy Relief in relation to, 101; communication as key to, 60; Dunkirk evacuation compared to, 53–54; improvisation and, 106–107; Loy reflecting on, 13; maritime radio for, 93, 95–96; of 9/11, 9–10; pareidolia impacting, 104; probability lessons and, 153; psychology and, 109; Rapp on, 46–47; simulated annealing in, 122, 123; social contracts and, 112–113, 114; transference dynamic role in, 44, 131; tugboat communities role in, 130–131. *See also* Loy, James
9/11: benchmarking and, limitations of, 53–54, 56; benchmarking paradox regarding, 9; cell phones on, use of, 95; Hobbes in relation to, 110; ICS on, problems with, 93, 94–95; New York Harbor rescue of, 9–10; Oklahoma City bombing compared to, 55; safety presentation points regarding, 137–138; situational awareness on, lack of, 31, 39; social contracts impacted by, 116; the torus in relation to, 22
NPBEA. *See* National Policy Board for Educational Administration

Oklahoma City bombing, 55, 148
Operation Frequent Wind, 134
outcomes: process over, focus on, 78, 79; simulated annealing and suboptimal, 122

paradox: benchmarking, 9; chaos, 91; safety, 27; safety systems, 92

pareidolia: New York Harbor rescue impacted by, 104; terminology for, 103; of the torus, 17; transference dynamic in relation to, 103, 103–104

parents: field trip denied by, 26; helicopter, 26, 27, 154, 154–155; restrictions on, 27; safety reassurance for, 12

Patriot Act: civilian rescue forces and, 100; Congress passing, 113–114; expansion of, 116

Pechon, Katie: Cajun Navy Relief working with, 100; ICS and, 100–101; on Internet, 101

performance variables, 92

planning: intuition/instincts over, 3; leadership and, 157–158

police: firefighters and EMS coordinating with, 97, 98; ICS used by, 94

politicians, 149

pop culture, 51

positionality: definition of, 74; as survey flaw, 75

positive recency effect, 75

power struggles, 111–112

"Prior Knowledge of Potential School-Based Violence: Information Students Learn May Prevent a Targeted Attack," 76

probability: helicopter parents and, 154; New York Harbor rescue and lessons in, 153; reasonable degree of, 135; simulated annealing as, 121

Professional Standards for Educational Leaders (PSEL): of NPBEA, 85; uselessness of, 86–87

projected benchmarking, 10–13

PSEL. *See* Professional Standards for Educational Leaders

psychology: New York Harbor rescue and, 109; of safety, 159

Puller, Lewis Burwell, 131

qualitative information gathering: after drills, 73–74; quantitative practices compared to, 74; School for the Blind using, 60

quantitative practices, 74

Rapp, Paul: as chaos theory expert, 119; as constructivist, 47; on heart rate variability, 142; mountain peak analogy of, 120; on transference dynamic, 46–47

report cards, 134

research, individual responder, 140–141

response rates, survey, 75

Riecker, Timothy, 96

Robber's Cave experiment, 113, 114, 127

rubber bullet drills, 66

safety: acceptable tolerances and, 21; equality as issue of, 46, 49; generations in relation to, differences between, 50–51; GIS for, 8; over liberty, 113–114; mantra, 5, 70, 142, 157–158; paradox, 27; presentation points, 137–138; psychology of, 159; reassurance of, following disaster, 12. *See also* drills; school safety

safety professionals: adaptability for, 40; empiricism and constructivism for, 47; paralyzation of, 39

safety systems: events impacting, changing dynamics of, 91; faculty/staff developing, 92; future preparation for, 138; group dynamics and, 109; introspection for improving, 139; intuition/instincts for, 3; on Loy, converging of, 119; paradox, 92; performance variables of, 92; reasoning for development of, 117

School for the Blind: fire at, 59–60; fire drills at, 59–60

school safety: benchmarking and, limitations of, 57; as billion dollar industry, 1, 6–7; bling, 50, 57; bollards for, 145–146, 147; common sense for, 150; discretion for, in-the-moment, 133; flower planter barriers for, 146; four pillars of knowledge regarding, 2–3; gun control legislation regarding, 143; insurance company assessment for, 7–9; intruder training for, 67; lawyers influencing, 154–155; legacy knowledge for, 129–130; politicians on, 149; presentation points on, 137–138; PSEL failure regarding, 85, 86–87;

report cards in relation to, 134; threat identification for, 148–149; the torus for, teaching of, 20; in 2030, 116

school shootings: craziness resulting from, 63; Dikkers on preventing, 84; FBI on, 1, 5; ICS for, 94; lack of data on, 4–5; leakage detection for preventing, 1; legislators response to, 143; positive recency effect and, 75; prevention of, connecting with students for, 84; rareness of, 82; social media posts prior to, 83; video games for training on, 81–82, 83–84; youth code of silence and, 76

Scouting Games (Baden-Powell), 32

self-awareness: of biases, 21–22; gut feelings in relation to, 30; induction process and, 158–159

self-preservation: as motivation, 122; over social contracts, 113

sensemaking: airplane pilots and, 132; distributed, 133–135; gut feelings and, 29, 30; process of, 29–30; for situational awareness, 30

Shah, N., 143

Sikh temple shooting, 97–98

simulated annealing: application of, 120–121; in chaos theory, 119, 120; for creative state, 122; engagement in, 121; irrationality to reason with, 123; metaphor, 119–120; in New York Harbor rescue, 122, 123; outcomes and, suboptimal, 122; as probability, 121; Rapp's mountain peak analogy for, 120

situational awareness: during drills, 30; gut feelings and, 29, 30; on 9/11, lack of, 31, 39; sensemaking for, 30; student exercises for enhancing, 31–32; the torus linked to, 2; value of, 141

situational discretion, 78

smartphones: focus lock from, 31; social contract with, 115; tribe, 45, 150; Zello Walkie Talkie app, 100

social contracts: dangers with, 114–115; Hobbes and, 112; New York Harbor rescue and, 112–113, 114; 9/11 impacting, 116; self-preservation over, 113; with smartphones, 115

social contract theory, 100

social media: Cajun Navy Relief helped by, 100; fears discussed on, 13; JTI on, 99; shooters posting intentions on, 83

soldiers: desensitization of, 83; drills for, 69; in Operation Frequent Wind, 134

the sovereign: Hobbes's concept of, 112; liberty given up to, 113; Loy emerging as, 113; superorganism compared to, 126

spatial memory, 121–122

Spillane, James, 133

staff. *See* faculty/staff

students: desensitization of, 64; with disabilities, 149; discipline data on, 150; discretion for best interests of, 134–135; drill buddy for engagement of, 65; enrollment of, 149; field trip denied to, 26; focus groups for, 150; natural leadership, ability to recognize, 45–46; natural light helping, 143; overpreparation as risk to, 1; schedules of, changing, 116; situational awareness exercises for, 31–32; social contract dangers for today's, 114–115; teachers and, connections between, 84; transference dynamic influencing, 159

Sullivan, Kevin, 69

superorganism concept, 126

surveys: for faculty/staff following drills, 70–71; flaws of using, 74–76

survival of the fittest: Darwin and, 125; leadership at odds with, 126

survivor math, 113

SWAT gear, 67

tabletop exercises: for engagement, 78; for improvement of judgment, 79; for process examination, 78; purpose of, 77; rules of, 77

teachers: discretion of, 134–135; fear of punishment, 131; ICS and, 96; immobilization of, 139; institutional memory of, 33; legacy knowledge for, 129–130; meltdown of, 70; shyness around improvisation, 132; students and, connections between, 84; video games for training, 81–82, 83–84; YouTube used by, 34

teaching objectives, 65

Tenth Amendment Center, 28
threat identification, 148–149
threat reporting: faculty/staff overworked
    from, 161; process of fixing, 161–163;
    suppression of, 149–150
Titanic, 105–106
tolerances, acceptable, 21
tornadoes: drills for, 63; JTI for, 99
the torus: baseline from, 30, 50; from chaos
    theory, 2; regarding comfort zones, 19;
    regarding disasters, 20, 23–24;
    familiarity bubble of, 139; legacy
    knowledge and, 34–35; metal detectors
    and, 139–140; 9/11 in relation to, 22;
    pareidolia of, 17; reasoning for, 17–18;
    teaching of, for school safety, 20;
    visualization for, 18–19
"The Trail Bollard Hazard," 147
transference dynamic: alphas and, 45;
    definition of, 43; faculty/staff and
    students influenced by, 159; gut
    feelings and, 44; during Hurricane
    Katrina, loss of, 100; microaggressions
    from, 46; in New York Harbor rescue,
    44, 131; pareidolia in relation to, 103,
    103–104; range of, 43–44; Rapp on,
    46–47; from social media, 100; trust
    from, 137
transparency, 138

Trump, Kenneth, 6
tugboat community, 130–131

Ujifusa, A., 143

Varian, Fred, 95
vehicle attacks, 145
video games: Dikkers on, 83–84; drills
    compared to, 82; survival skills over,
    basic, 84; for teacher training, 81–82,
    83–84
Vietnam, 134
virtual field trip, 27

War of the Worlds, 115
Webster, Daniel, 143
Weick, K. E., 29
what3words global addressing system, 158
Williams, Genevieve, 99
Williams, Rebecca, 99
World Trade Center: 1993 bombing of, 3;
    structural resilience of, 141. *See also*
    9/11

youth code of silence: parents complicit in,
    26; school shootings and, 76
YouTube, 34

Zello Walkie Talkie, 100

About the Author

Credit: Fred Galley.

David P. Perrodin, PhD, promotes a safety initiative of taking action before a disaster strikes. He is an author, educator, researcher, professor, expert witness, consultant, host of *The Safety Doc* podcast, and bicyclist. David received his Doctorate of Philosophy in Educational Leadership and Policy Analysis at University of Wisconsin-Madison, where he researched high-stakes safety decisions in education, health care, and military. He has presented on PBS and wrote and directed a film about school safety with Pulitzer Prize–winner David Obst. Dr. Perrodin has a passion for helping schools and companies design and implement safety instruction and threat-reporting tools that are accessible to students with special needs.

Lightning Source UK Ltd.
Milton Keynes UK
UKHW041151150819
348010UK00002B/444/P

9 781475 837445